Bible
Yo

EXODUS

Leaving Behind, Moving On

Barbara K. Mittman

Abingdon Press
Nashville

Exodus: Leaving Behind, Moving On

20/30: Bible Study for Young Adults

by Barbara K. Mittman

Copyright © 1999 by Abingdon Press

ISBN 0-687-08308-7

This book is printed on acid-free paper.

Manufactured in the United States of America.

00 01 02 03 04 05 06 07 08—10 9 8 7 6 5 4 3 2

CONTENTS

MEET THE WRITER

Barbara K. Mittman is an ordained deacon, certified in Christian education and youth ministry. She currently serves as the Iowa Conference Youth Coordinator and with First United Methodist Church in Nevada, Iowa. Barb has previously published church school curriculum for youth. Barb, her husband Bob, and daughter Katie live in Nevada, Iowa.

WELCOME TO 20/30:
BIBLE STUDY
FOR YOUNG ADULTS

The *20/30* Bible study series is offered for post-modern adults who want to participate in and help structure their own discoveries—in life, in relationships, in faith. In each of the volumes of this series, we will have the opportunity to use our own experience in life and faith to examine the biblical texts in new ways. We will examine biblical images that shape all of our lives, even if we are not immediately aware that they do.

Image Is Everything

Images are what shape our decisions. We may think or know certain important data that weigh heavily in a decision. We may value the advice and counsel of others. We may find that the stated or implied wishes of others influence what we do. But in the end, it is often the *image* we hold that makes the decision.

For example, perhaps you were deeply hurt by someone important to you—an employer, a friend, even a pastor. You know in your heart that the institution is not to blame or that friendships are based on more than one event. But the image shaped by the difficult experience is that the job, or the friend, or the church cannot be relied upon. You *know* better, but you just have to make a change anyway. The image was more powerful than the reason.

Images are powerful, and they are familiar. In each of the studies in this series, you will encounter a well-known image that will connect your familiar experiences with some basis in Scripture.

You know what it is like to move to a new place, to have to deal with transitions in school or work or in relationships. You have probably experienced changes in your family as you have grown up and moved out on your own. Some of these moves are gradual, just taken in stride. Others can be painful or abrupt; certainly life-changing. In *Exodus: Leaving Behind, Moving On*, you will appreciate learning how God is in the midst of those movements, no matter how minor or how transformational.

You know what it's like to make agreements, to establish commitments, to give your word and expect to be trusted. *Covenant: Making Commitments That Count* engages you in study sessions that explain a variety of covenants, what happens when covenants are broken, how to have a faithful covenant to care for others and for the earth, and certainly, what it means to have this sacred covenant with God.

You know how important it is to have a sense of support and roots; to have friends and a life partner. *Community: Living Faithfully With Others* introduces you to Scriptures and life examples that delve into intimacy, work, family relationships, and more.

You have faith, but may also realize that it can mean many things. Is it belief or trust or waiting or moral behavior or something else? Or it is all those things? *Faith: Living a Spiritual Life* helps you examine your faith and grow as a Christian.

Experience, Faith, Growth, and Action

Each volume in this series will help you probe, on your own terms, how your experience links with your faith and how deepening your faith develops your life experience. If you need a prompt for your reflection, each volume has several pages of real life case studies. As your faith and commitment to Jesus Christ grow, you may be looking for ways to be involved in specific service opportunities. Several are listed on page 80.

We hope this series will help you encounter God through Scripture, reflection, and dialogue with others who desire to grow in faith and to serve others. One image we hold is that God is in all things. God is certainly with you.

HOW TO USE THIS RESOURCE

Each session of this resource includes similar components or elements:
- A statement of the issue or question to be explored
- Several "voices" of persons who are currently dealing with that issue
- Exploration of biblical passages relative to the question raised
- "Bible 101" boxes that provide insight about the study of the Bible
- Questions for reflection and discussion
- Suggested individual and group activities designed to bring the session to life
- Optional case studies (found in the back of the book)
- Various service learning activities related to the session (found in the back of the book)

Choices, Choices, Choices

Collectively, these components mean one thing: *choice*. You have choices to make concerning how to use each session of this resource. Want just the nitty-gritty Bible reading, reflection, and study for personal or group use? Then focus your attention on just those components during your study time.

Like starting with real-life stories about issues then moving into how the Bible might be relevant? Start with the "voices" and move on from there. Use the "voices" to encourage group members to speak about their own experiences.

Prefer highly charged discussion encounters where many different viewpoints can be heard? Start the session with the biblical passages, followed by the questions and group activities. Be sure to compare the ideas found in the "Bible 101" boxes with your current ideas for more discussion. Want the major challenge of applying biblical principles to a difficult problem? After reading the biblical material, read one of the case studies, using the guidelines provided on page 14, or get involved with one of the service learning options, described on 80.

Great Versatility

This resource has been designed for many different uses. Some persons will use this resource for personal study and reflection. Others will want to explore the work with a small group of friends. And still other folks will see this book as a different type of Sunday school resource.

Spend some time thinking about your own questions, study habits, and learning styles or those of your small group. Then use the guidelines mentioned above to fashion each session into a unique Bible study session to meet those requirements.

Highly Participatory

As you will see, the Scriptures, "voices," commentary, and experience of group members will provide an opportunity for an active, engaging time together. The greatest challenge for a group leader might be "crowd control"—being sure everyone has the chance to put his or her ideas into the mix!

The Scriptures will help you and those who study with you to make connections between real-life issues and the Bible. This resource values and encourages personal participation as a means to fully understand and appreciate the intersection of personal belief with God's ongoing work in each and every life.

ON ORGANIZING A SMALL GROUP

Learning with a small group of persons offers certain advantages over studying by yourself. First, you will hopefully encounter different opinions and ideas, making the experience of Bible study a richer and more challenging event. Second, any leadership responsibilities can be shared among group members. Third, different persons will bring different talents. Some will be deep thinkers while other group members will be creative giants. Some persons will be newcomers to the Bible; their questions and comments will help others clarify their deeply held assumptions.

So how does one go about forming a small group? Follow the steps below and see how easy this task can be.

- **Read through the resource carefully.** Think about the ideas presented, the questions raised, and the exercises suggested. If the sessions of this work excite you, it will be easier for you to spread your enthusiasm to others.

- **Spend some time thinking about church members, friends, and co-workers who might find the sessions of this resource interesting**. On a sheet of paper, list two characteristics or talents you see in each person that would make him or her an attractive Bible study group member. Some talents might include "deep thinker," "creative wizard," or "committed Christian." Remember: the best small group has members who differ in learning styles, talents, ideas, and convictions, but who respect the dignity and integrity of the other members.

- **Most functional small groups have seven to fifteen members.** Make a list of potential group members that doubles your target number. For instance, if you would like a small group of seven to ten members, be prepared to invite fourteen to twenty persons.

- **Once your list of potential candidates is complete, decide on a tentative location and time.** Of course, the details can be negotiated with those persons who accept the invitation, but you need to sound definitive and clear to prospective group members. "We will initially set Wednesday night from 7 to 9 P.M. at my house for our meeting time" will sound more attractive than "Well, I don't know either when or where we would be meeting, but I hope you will consider joining us."

- **Make initial contact with prospective group members short, sweet, and to the point.** Say something like, "We are putting together a Bible study using a different kind of resource. When would be a good time to show you the resource and talk about the study?" Establishing a special time to make the invitation takes the pressure off the prospective group member to make a quick decision.

- **Show up at the decided time and place.** Talk with each prospective member individually. Bring a copy of the resource with you. Show each person what excites you about the study and mention the two unique characteristics or talents you feel he or she would offer the group. Tell each person the initial meeting time and location and how many weeks the small group will meet. Also mention that the need for a new time or location could be discussed during the first group meeting. Ask for a commitment to come to the first session. Thank individuals for their time.

- **Give a quick phone call or email to thank all persons for their consideration and interest.** Remind persons of the time and location of the first meeting.

- **Be organized.** Use the first group meeting to get acquainted. Briefly describe the seven sessions. Have a book for each group member, and discuss sharing responsibilities for leadership.

LEADING AND
SHARING LEADERSHIP

So the responsibility to lead the group has fallen on you? Don't sweat it. Follow these simple suggestions and you will razzle and dazzle the group with your expertise.

- **Read the session carefully.** Look up all the Bible passages. Take careful notes about the ideas, statements, questions, and activities in the session. Try all the activities.

- **Using twenty to twenty-five blank index cards, write one idea, activity, Bible passage, or question from the session on each card** until you either run out of material or cards. Be sure to look at the case studies and service learning options. Number the cards so they will follow the order of the session.

- **Spend a few moments thinking about the members of your group.** How many like to think about ideas, concepts, or problems? How many need to "feel into" an idea by storytelling, worship, prayer, or group activities? Who are the "actors" who prefer a hands-on or participatory approach, such as an art project or simulation, to grasp an idea? List the names of all group members, and record whether you believe each to be THINKER, FEELER, or ACTOR.

- **Place all the index cards in front of you in the order in which they originally appeared in the session.** Looking at that order, ask yourself: (1) Where is the "Head" of the session—the key ideas or concepts? (2) Where is the "Heart" of the session in which persons will have a deep feeling response? (3) Where are the "feet"—those activities that ask the group to put the ideas and feelings to use? Separate the cards into three stacks: HEAD, HEART, and FEET.

- **Now construct the "body" for your class.** Shift the cards around, using a balance of HEAD, HEART, and FEET cards to determine which activities you will do and in what order. This will be your group's unique lesson plan. Try to choose as many cards as you have group members. Then, match the cards: HEAD and THINKERS; HEART and FEELERS; FEET and ACTORS for each member of the group. Don't forget a card for yourself. For instance, if your group has ten members, you should have about ten cards.

- **Develop the leadership plan.** Invite group members prior to the session to assist in the leadership. Show them the unique lesson plan you developed. Ask for their assistance in developing and/or leading each segment of the session as well as an introduction and a closing ritual or worship experience.

Your lesson plan should start with welcoming the participants. Hopefully everyone will have read the session ahead of time. Then, begin to move through the activity cards in the order of your unique session plan, sharing the leadership as you have agreed.

You may have chosen to have all the HEAD activities together, followed by the HEART cards. This would introduce the session's content, followed by helping group members "feel into" the issue through interactive stories, questions, and exercises with all group members. Feel free to add more storytelling, discussion, prayer, meditation, or worship.

You may have chosen to use the FEET cards to end the session. Ask the group, "What difference should this session make in our daily lives?" You or the ACTORS should introduce the FEET cards as possible ways to discern a response. Ensuring that group members leave with a few practical suggestions for doing something different during the week is the point of this section of the unique lesson plan.

- **Remember: leading the group does not mean "Do it all yourself."** With a little planning, you can enlist the talents of many group members. By inviting group members to lead parts of the session that feel comfortable for them, you will model and encourage shared leadership. Welcome their interests in music, prayer, worship, Bible, and so on, to develop innovative and creative Bible study sessions that can transform lives in the name of Jesus Christ.

CHOOSING TEACHING OPTIONS

This young adult series was designed, written, and produced out of an understanding of the attributes, concerns, joys, and faith issues of young adults. With great care and integrity, this image-based print resource was developed to connect biblical events and relationships with contemporary, real-life situations of young adults. Its pages will promote Christian relationships and community, support new biblical learning, encourage spiritual development, and empower faithful decision-making and action.

This study is well-suited to young adults and may be used confidently and effectively. But with the great diversity within the young adult population, not every line of this study will be written "just for you." To be most relevant, some portions of the study material need to be tailored to fit your particular group. Adjustments for a good fit involve making choices from options offered by the resource. This customizing may be done easily by a designated leader who is familiar with the layout of the resource and the young adults who are using it.

What to Expect

In this study, Scripture and real-life images mesh together to provoke a personal response. Young adults will find themselves thinking, feeling, imagining, questioning, making decisions, professing faith, building connections, inviting discipleship, taking action, and making a difference. Scripture is at the core of each session. Scenarios weave in the dimensions of real life. Narrative and text boxes frame plenty of teaching options to offer young adults.

Each session is part of a cohesive volume, but is designed to stand alone. One session is not dependent on knowledge or experience accumulated from other sessions. A group leader can freely choose from the teaching options in an individual session without wondering about how it might affect the other sessions.

A Good Fit

For a better fit, alter the session based on what is known about the young adult participants. Young adults are a diverse constituency with varied experiences, interests, needs, and values. There is really no single defining characteristic that links young adults. Specific information about the age, employment status, household, personal relationships, and lifestyle among participants will equip a leader to make choices that ensure a good fit.

■ **Customize.** Read through the session. Notice how scenarios and teaching options move from integrating Scripture and real-life dimensions to inviting a response.

■ **Look at the scenario(s).** How real is the presentation of real life? Say that the main character is a professional, white male, married, in his upper twenties, and caught in a workplace dilemma that entangles his immediate superior and a subordinate from his division. Perhaps your group members are mostly college students and recent graduates, unmarried, and still on the way to being "settled." There are many differences between the man in the scenario and these group members.

As a leader, you could choose to eliminate the case study, substitute it with another scenario (there are several more choices on pages 75–79), claim the validity of the dilemma, and shift the spotlight from the main character to the subordinate, or modify the description of the main character. Break-Out groups based on age or employment experience might also be used to accommodate the differences and offer a better fit.

■ **Look at the teaching options.** How are the activities propelling participants toward a personal response? Perhaps the Scripture study requires more meditative quiet than is possible and a more academic, verbal, or artistic approach would offer a better fit. Maybe more direct decisions or actions would fit better than more passive or logical means. Try to keep a balance, though, that allows participants to "get out of their head" to reflect and also to move toward action.

Conceivably, there could just be too much in any one session. As a leader, you can pick and choose among teaching options, substitute case studies, take two meetings to do one session, and adapt any process to make a better fit. The tailoring process can be evaluated as adjustments are made. Judge the fit every time you meet. Ask questions that gauge relevance, and assess how the resource has stretched minds, encouraged discipleship, and changed lives.

USING BREAK-OUT GROUPS

20/30 Break-Out groups are small groups that encourage the personal sharing of lives and the gospel. The name "Break-Out" is a sweeping term that includes a variety of small group settings. A Break-Out group may resemble a Bible study group, an interest group, a sharing group, or other types of Christian fellowship groups.

Break-Out groups offer young adults a chance to belong and personally relate to one another. Members are known, nurtured, and heard by others. Young adults may agree and disagree while maximizing the exchange of ideas, information, or options. They might explore, confront, and resolve personal issues and feelings with empathy and support. Participants can challenge and hold each other accountable to a personalized faith and stretch its links to real life and service.

Forming Break-Out Groups

The nature of these small Break-Out groups will depend on the context and design of the specific session. On occasion the total group of participants will be divided for a particular activity. Break-Out groups will differ from one session to the next. Variations may involve the size of the group, how group members are divided, or the task of the group. Break-Out groups may also be used to accommodate differences and help tailor the session plan for a better fit. In some sessions, specific group assembly instructions will be provided. For other sessions, decisions regarding the size or division of small groups will be made by the designated leader. Break-Out groups may be in the form of pairs or trios, family-sized groups of three to six members, or groups of up to ten members.

They may be arranged simply by grouping persons seated next to one another or in more intentional ways by common interests, characteristics, or life experience. Consider creating Break-Out groups according to age; gender; type of household, living arrangements, or love relationships; vocation, occupation, career, or employment status; common or built-in connections; lifestyle; values or perspective; or personal interests or traits.

Membership

The membership of Break-Out groups will vary from session to session, or even within specific sessions. Young adults need to work at knowing and being known, so that there can be a balance between Break-Out groups that are more similar and those that reflect greater diversity. There may be times when more honest communication, trust, or accountability may be desired and group leaders will need to be free to self-select members for small groups.

It is important for *20/30* Break-Out groups to practice acceptance and to value the worth of others. The potential for small groups to encourage personal sharing and significant relationships is enhanced when members agree to exercise active listening skills, keep confidences, expect authenticity, foster trust, and develop ways of loving one another. All group members contribute to the development and function of Break-Out groups. Designated leaders especially need to model manners of hospitality and help ensure that each group member is respected.

Invitational Listening

Consider establishing an "invitational listening" routine that validates the perspective and affirms the voice of each group member. After a question or statement is posed, pause and allow time to think—not all persons think on their feet or talk out loud to think. Then, initiate conversation by inviting one group member, by name, to talk. This person may either choose to talk or to "pass." Either way, this person is honored and is offered an opportunity to speak and be heard. This person carries on the ritual by inviting another group member, by name, to speak. The process continues until all have been invited, by name, to talk. As each one invites another, the responsibility of acceptance and hospitality in the Break-Out groups is shared among all its members.

Study group members Break-Out to belong, to share the gospel, to care, and to watch over one another in Christian love. "So deeply do we care for you that we are determined to share with you not only the gospel of God but also our own selves, because you have become very dear to us" (1 Thessalonians 2:8).

EXODUS:
LEAVING BEHIND, MOVING ON

Exodus is a way out. It is a decisive act to leave behind and move on. The journey is epic. The story of self-preservation folds in on itself and vacillates between jubilant celebration and bitter despair. The trek is marked by life-giving action and events and episodes of wandering, suffering, and grace.

The Exodus

Exodus was a way out of bondage, a call that tore the Israelites out of Egypt. In the Bible, the Book of Exodus tells of a people who leave behind Egypt and the bondage of Pharaoh and move on to freedom and life in a land promised by God. In between Egypt and the Promised Land were years of wilderness wandering and life marked by miracles, murmuring, mourning, and metamorphosis. The story tells of lives embraced by an active and present God. The experience provides a way to interpret the whole history of God's people—from the promises of Abraham to the promises of God for you today.

This is a powerful story and an enduring one. Take a minute to think about the context. The Israelites migrated to Egypt because there was a severe famine in the land God had given to them through the promise to Abraham. Their first exodus was to leave the Promised Land (which at the time didn't show much promise) for a foreign place (whose second in command was an Israelite). The good times lasted a long while, but then went sour. A new ruler came to power and put the Israelites into slavery.

Moses was called by God to go to Egypt, to announce to Pharaoh that the people were to be released, and then to lead them back to the Promised Land. Moses tried five different excuses to get out of this task. God got exasperated, and Moses ran out of excuses. (See Exodus 3–4.) When Moses petitioned Pharaoh, Pharaoh either turned him down or said yes then changed his mind. (This sounds more like last year's company board meeting than a Bible story!)

When the people were finally freed, they were pursued by Pharaoh's army; but once again God provided a way out. Now they were finally freedom bound. And what did the people do while they traveled through the desert to what would be the land of their inheritance? They griped, incessantly. "It's too long." "It's too hot." "There's no food; at least in Egypt we had our veggies to eat." "Why did you bring us out here to die?" That enslavement looked pretty enticing after all—the "better the devil you know than the devil you don't" philosophy.

Can you see yourself in that picture? The point is, exodus events take courage, cooperation, willingness to brave the unknown, flexibility, and at least a modest amount of humor.

What Is Your Own Exodus?

How is this image and experience of exodus relevant? Sometimes the way out is dictated by family traditions, social customs, or achievements—college after high school; on the job, out of the house, and on your own after college; or stepping up the corporate ladder. Some experiences demand a clean break—violent personal relationships, substance abuse, or persecution. Other movings on may only be temporary or transitory—a summer at home, an internship, or part-time employment. Some leaving behind promises great rewards—a new job, marriage, or military service. Others offer nothing but a chance to escape—invasive medical treatment, refugee resettlement, or even death. Sometimes the way out is obvious. Other decisions to leave behind and move on are more ambiguous and require a great deal of soul-searching. Even the desired, expected, and anticipated exodus moments can be difficult and anxiety-producing.

Exodus and wilderness experiences significantly define the identity and existence of communities and individuals. How important have decisions to leave behind and move on been in your life? Pick such a decision and candidly judge the impact it had on your life. How has your identity been shaped by this experience? Chances are, you would not be who you are right now if it were not for your exodus decisions and wilderness experiences.

Exodus Treks as Transformation

The decision to leave behind and move on begs for change. In the context and language of Christian faith, believers use the words *saved, blessed, pardoned, redeemed, delivered, liberated, forgiven,* and *loved* to talk about our hope for the end of an exodus trek. We talk about transformation that is made possible by the life-giving, life-preserving, and life-blessing action of God. In the same way that God transformed the Israelites from slaves to a people free to serve God, we can move on as God's chosen and beloved people, too.

Leave behind, and move on your own exodus trek. Watch your own progress on your own journey. Take your place as a character in this chronicle of God's way with God's people.

GOT TO GO

This session is designed to claim the need for exodus, characterize these treks, and point to the defining potential of exodus experiences.

GETTING STARTED

Exodus is a way out. It is a decisive act that leaves behind and moves on. In between a departure and an arrival is a journey that can significantly define the identity and existence of an individual, household, community, or nation.

Departures are those defining moments when it is time to go. Some are dictated by family traditions or social customs—like going away to college right after high school. Abusive situations demand a clean break. New starts, such as a job, marriage, or pregnancy, promise great rewards. A crack in the wall may be big enough for a refugee to escape. Sometimes walking out requires a great deal of soul-searching. Other decisions to take off are plain and clear.

Make a two-column chart similar to the Departure/Arrival schedules you see in mass transit stations and in airports. Put "Departures" at the top of the left column and "Arrivals" at the top of the right. Generate a list of exodus departure times. Record them in the left-column under "Departures."

Getting Started
Make introductions.
Get acquainted by providing each other with personal and identifying information, such as age, family relationships, employment status, and leisure interests.

Make the "Departure and Arrival" list described in the text. What are the most typical examples of departures in your life? (Do not deal with arrivals or fill in that side of the chart. It will be done in Session 7.)

GOD DELIVERS

God Delivers
Read Exodus 3:1-12.
God was made visible in a blazing bush. Moses investigated. How did God approach Moses and what did Moses do? Has God done something dramatic to get your attention? If so, what happened? When has your inquiring mind led you to God?

What does it take for exodus to become a viable possibility for those who suffer?

Describe a time when you have heard cries of suffering. How did you struggle with the decision to get involved? How did you clarify the task and your role?

God was revealed to Moses. God heard the cries of the oppressed in Egypt. God promised to deliver. Moses was sent by God to do what Israel could not do itself (Exodus 3:1-12).

The goal was the removal of the Israelites from slavery in Egypt. God's people would be delivered from their misery and brought ". . . up out of that land to a good and broad land, a land flowing with milk and honey" (Exodus 3:8). Moses was sent by God to Pharaoh to bring the Israelites out of Egypt. But Moses could not liberate alone.

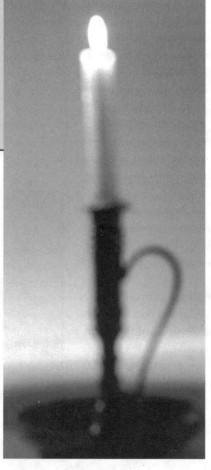

Moses' curiosity about the burning bush led to his call. Even after seeing and hearing the divine, Moses really struggled from this initial privilege to respond. In the span of just seven verses, Moses shifted from a ready "Here I am" to a reluctant "Who am I?" Moses questioned his own abilities to bring the people out of Egypt, but God promised to be with him.

This is not just a heroic extrication! God's people are not just plucked out of adverse situations. Deliverance brings the assurance of divine presence and the promise of new life.

Theresa

Theresa walked out on her partner's regular battering and verbal abuse. Theresa had been less than willing to leave, and her reluctance had made her exodus a long time coming.

Theresa
This is a Moses exodus. Invite a volunteer to begin with the details about Theresa in the text and to continue the story. After a sentence or two, have someone else pick up the story.

Who heard Theresa's cries? Who saved her? How was she rescued? What is promised by this act of deliverance?

C A S E STUDY

Sit With the Word
Look at the remaining biblical texts for this session (Bible boxes), and check out how each character (Michelle, Stefan, Brian, and Kole) makes his or her move to go. (You will look at their situations again in Session 7 in terms of arrival.) You may choose to spend time with the Scripture individually, in pairs, or in small groups. Explore all the texts or choose the one that connects most closely with your own experience that follows the Exodus move of the Israelites. If you prefer, divide the texts among "Break-Out" groups.

Use these questions as discussion starters:
- What are the consequences of leaving behind? results of moving on?
- What does it take for exodus to become a viable possibility?
- What are the connections between faithful living, leaving behind, and moving on?

DISCUSS

SIT WITH THE WORD

Michelle is chosen to play ball for a university two thousand miles from home. Stefan is caught hiding behind a claim of wealth, a lavish lifestyle, and a pile of credit cards. Brian and his family are forced to leave their home when an explosion and fire ravage his neighborhood. Kole is accused of sexually abusing a young woman.

Michelle is called out. Stefan is found out. Brian is forced out. Kole is led out. Each is an exodus.

THE PROMISE OF GREAT REWARDS

God told Abram to go from his country to a land that God would show him. God promised to make Abram a great nation, to make his name great, and to bless him. Assured of his family's survival and an identity as a person of faith, Abram went (Genesis 12:1-9).

Abram abandoned his homeland and relinquished his own ancestral bonds. His decision to go was a faithful response to God's promises of offspring and land. In spite of the obvious realities—his age, Sarai's barrenness, and the Canaanite occupation of the land he was promised—Abram left.

God presumed nothing, but offered everything. The one without potential was chosen. God said, "I will . . ."; and Abram said, "Yes!" What did not even exist before will now flourish. Out of hopelessness will come life.

Michelle

Michelle was chosen to play ball for a university two thousand miles from home. She was called by a coach who promised a full-ride scholarship and graduation as a student athlete. But, Michelle is unqualified as an athlete and a student. Michelle never started a high school varsity game. Her grade point aver-

BIBLE

**Promise of Reward
Read Genesis 12:1-9.**
What was Abram asked to do? What did it mean for him and his family? Is that something you think you could do? Explain.

CASE STUDY

Michelle
This is an Abram exodus. Does Michelle go or say "No"? Play out the consequences of either decision. When does a decision like this become a matter of life or death?

age, class rank, and college placement exam scores make her ineligible for most scholarships.

HIDING OUT

Episodes of hiding dominate the story of the prophet Elijah. Elijah has promised a drought to show that it is his God, the God of Israel—not the god Baal—who controlled the rain (1 Kings 17:1-7). God commanded Elijah to flee and hide himself from King Ahab and Queen Jezebel. Elijah had to hide to protect God's purposes. Through it all, the word of God was the prime mover and Elijah "went and did" (17:5) in obedience. Eventually Elijah would speak the word that would bring life-giving rain to a drought-stricken land.

BIBLE

Hiding Out
Read I Kings 17:1-7.
Elijah declares the drought in response to the wickedness and faithlessness of the king. If Elijah was working for God, why, do you think, did he have to hide out? Why is doing God's work sometimes risky? What was at stake for Elijah? for Israel? for the king?

LOOK CLOSER

Look Closer
Read 1 Kings 16:29–18:6 and a Bible commentary on this passage. What are the hardships endured by the few characters we see in this passage? Why has it gone on so long? What brings events to a head? Where is God in the midst of the trials of these people? What message is there here for you?

Stefan

Ever since leaving home after college, Stefan has hidden behind a claim of wealth, a lavish lifestyle, and a pile of credit cards. This past year, Stefan married Alise and together they have become quite accustomed to spending well beyond their means; having a savings account never entered their heads. Alise has even learned how to use the "finer things in life" as a lever in their relationship and frequently pressures Stefan into spending exorbitant amounts of money to keep her happy. Their income has long since dried-up, collection agencies are calling, and options are in short supply.

CASE STUDY

Stefan
This is an Elijah exodus. But, Stefan can no longer hide. His house of (credit) cards is beginning to fall, and he needs to make a move. What options are available to Stefan? What real choices does he have? Assess each possibility in terms of its outcome on his lifestyle, on his wife, and on his integrity. What possible faith issues emerge here? Where might you see God at work here?

GONE JUST AWHILE

An angel of the Lord appeared to Joseph in a dream and instructed him to get up, to take Jesus and Mary to Egypt, and to remain there until they were told otherwise. They fled and remained in Egypt until the death of Herod, whose violence could have meant death for the infant Jesus. Later, the angel would appear again to authorize their return to the land of Israel, though not without a detour of its own (Matthew 2:13-15, 19-23).

Joseph picked up his family, took leave into Egypt, and awaited notice so they might return. For a time, Joseph and his family were refugees in Egypt. Although temporary, this exodus is defining. Jesus would not have been who he was without this exodus experience. The Son of God was saved and prophecy fulfilled.

Brian

Brian and his family are forced to flee their home when an explosion and fire ravage his neighborhood. Even as they were being evacuated to safe shelter, Brian knew they would be back.

LET US BE GOING

Jesus and the disciples went into a place called Gethsemane. Jesus was distressed and troubled. In the garden, he sought communion with God in prayer. In spite of Jesus' repeated requests that they stay up and sit with him, the disciples slept. Things were heating up, and Jesus was left in the garden to struggle alone. Promises were broken. He was deserted and betrayed by persons who were his closest friends and associates (Mark 14:32-50).

Jesus came to Simon Peter and to the others a third time, roused them, and said, "Get up, let us be going" (14:42). The handwriting was on the wall. The hour had come. Jesus left the garden to face his betrayer. First the kiss, then the arrest, and then abandonment.

Let Us Be Going
Read Mark 14:32-50. Why is Jesus in the garden? What do the disciples do (or not do)? What is the consequence? Where is God's presence evident?

Kole

Kole was accused of sexually abusing a young woman. The company misconduct policy allowed him to continue to work, but his relationships and movement were closely monitored. Kole was threatened with civil and criminal charges. More and more of his friends and family members deserted him. After much deliberation, Kole moved to accept an offer to meet the accuser with a mediator. He went in good faith, but was not surprised to see an arrest warrant on the table. Kole was read his rights, cuffed, and led out, alone.

Kole
This is a garden exodus. What might be next, beyond Kole's arrest? Is he further abandoned, or is he defended by friends and family? How might incarceration, probation, or acquittal trigger an exodus for Kole?

Look Closer
Using any of the four characters and Scripture passages, plan a brief demonstration that connects the Scripture to the scenario character and interprets that exodus time.

Demonstrations offer a lot of attitude and freedom to re-present circumstances and identities in ways that are meaningful to the persons involved. A demonstration might act out the event of the Scripture, but it could also be a speech or a game, a mime or some other ingenious re-telling, or even a pop quiz! Demonstrations encourage persons to make meaning in creative, clever, and inventive ways.

Present each demonstration. Compare the different scenarios. Claim any common links between faithful living, leaving behind, and moving on.

FUSING THE WORD AND MY WORLD

Think about your own story. Characterize your own exodus. See how your experience connects with the Scripture narratives. Interpret the consequences and results of leaving behind and moving on in your life.

Invite the others to tell their stories, witness to promises of hope and change, ask questions, or claim new understandings.

GOING FORTH

For Moses, for Abram and Sarai, for Elijah, for Joseph, and for Jesus, God's promises were the "go" behind the "got to go." God promised to guide an initially reluctant leader. God promised land and offspring. God promised life in the midst of death. God promised safety to a refugee family. God promised to be present at the time of trial.

Close with a litany of promise that alternates between the belief of a psalmist and God's promises for your life. Jot down your own "God promised . . ." statements.

Start with the words of the psalmist (Psalm 12:6a):

"The promises of the LORD are promises that are pure."

Then, offer one of your own "God promised . . ." statements. Together, respond with the words of the psalmist.

Continue to fashion this litany by alternating between your "God promised . . ." statements and the words of promise from Psalm 12.

Fusing the Word
Use these questions to integrate the cases (of the characters or of your own) with the scriptural examples of exodus moments.

When have you known that you just had to go? What did it take for this exodus to become a real option? Who or what was left behind? What was gained by moving on? Was your move most like Moses and the Israelites, Abram, Elijah, Joseph, or most like Jesus after his night in the garden? How was your experience similar? How do you connect this move with your own spiritual growth or faith story?

No one is obligated to share personal stories. If there is that level of openness, be ready to love, accept, and value others. Seek to understand, ask questions to clarify, honor differences, keep confidences, expect authenticity, foster trust, and resist the temptation to counsel. Model manners of hospitality that validate each one's voice and affirm them as persons of sacred worth.

Going Forth
What promises are the "go" behind your "got to go" times?

Take a moment to jot down your own "God promised . . ." statements. Offer each as a part of the litany of promise.

Exodus: Leaving Behind, Moving On

LEAVE-TAKING

This session is designed to explore leaving and to characterize how that happens.

GETTING STARTED

Three questions:
- Where are the places you have you lived?
- What is the longest time you have lived in one place?
- How did you get here, to this place?

Getting Started
Greet each other. Welcome and identify any new-comers. Invite each other to offer a brief, "life since we last met" update.

DISPLACED, DELIVERED, OR DEPLOYED?

Leave-taking might be best character-ized by the words *displaced, delivered*, or *deployed*.

Displaced, Delivered, or Deployed?
- *Displaced* alludes to an unex-pected, forced movement that might involve physical removal, dismissal, eviction, or expul-sion.
- *Delivered* implies being set free or liberated.
- *Deployed* suggests some inten-tional or strategic position or arrangement.

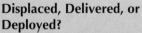

Susan

Susan

Work through Susan's story. There are at least ten different leave-taking events in Susan's story. Identify and mark them. Then, decide if each move is best characterized by the word *displaced, delivered*, or *deployed*.

If you prefer, use one of the cases on pages 75–79 or a personal experience of your own.

When Susan turned sixteen, her new driver's license was her ticket to freedom—coming and going to school and work with friends. Sue celebrated her graduation from high school and left home the following fall for a private four-year, liberal arts college. She trained as a teacher, traveled, spent summers away from home, declined a marriage proposal, and accepted her first job just ahead of graduation.

Days later, Sue moved into her first apartment with a friend from college and commuted to her new job. The job paid enough, offered health benefits, and had lots of creative potential. Her boss was authoritative, controlling, and more parental than collegial.

The next few years brought a quick succession of moves for Susan. After economic

and lifestyle disputes with her roommate, Sue moved into her own apartment. A few months later, she left her first job to go to graduate school. Sue enrolled mid-year and settled-in. Three terms later she was carrying a full load and working as an intern when she was suspended from her program of study. Now, more than two years after this academic "time-out," Susan has worked at a couple of other jobs, gone through several different living arrangements, and made the decision not to go back to grad school.

SIT WITH THE WORD

Displaced

When Abram and his extended family were called out of Ur, they journeyed together for some time, then parted company. Abram advanced toward Canaan; Lot headed to the "cities of the plain" and settled in Sodom. Lot's unfortunate choice of settlement witnesses to God's power to do beginnings and endings.

Sometime after Lot settled in, the depravity of the city came to God's notice. Lot was prodded by angels to flee the impending destruction. He lingered so long that the angels were provoked to seize him. A reluctant and resistant Lot was *displaced* unwillingly outside the city. Once there, it seemed as if Lot was already suffering his wife's fate—he could not flee (Genesis 19:12-29). Petrified by all his fear, Lot was saved by God's promise to Abraham (Genesis 18:22-33).

Two of the three angels who had visited with Abraham (18:1-15) went on to Sodom to investigate the reports of its wickedness. The third, generally understood to be God,

 BIBLE

Displaced
Read Genesis 19:12-29. How does this narrative illustrate displacement? How do you see God in the midst of it? Compare this description with a more recent case of displacement.

Read Exodus 6:1; 11:1; and 12:29-42. How do the actions of Pharaoh and the Egyptians depict displacement? Where do you see God's activity in these events?

Focus on a personal or current in-the-news leave-taking situation. Interpret the leaving from each of its distinct perspectives.

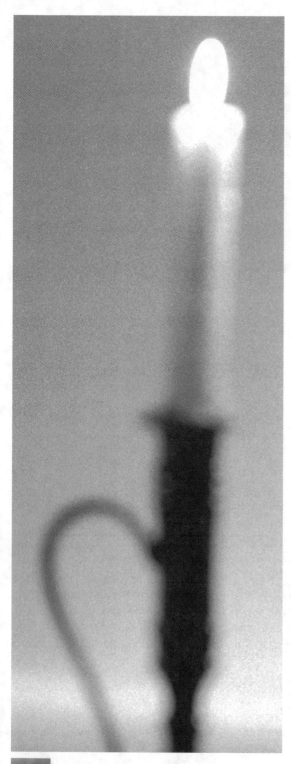

remained to speak with Abraham. It was at this time that Abraham realized that Sodom, the city of his nephew Lot, would be destroyed. This is the first instance of God displacing from the land an entire people.

To save Lot, Abraham boldly bargained with God, who relented several times until God agreed to spare the whole city for the sake of just ten righteous residents. Presumably, there were fewer than ten—Lot's family of four and his future sons-in-law, who chose not to leave—because the city was destroyed, but only after securing Lot's safety.

Many generations later, God expected the Israelites to be *displaced* and driven out of Egypt by Pharaoh himself. With a mighty hand, Pharaoh would ultimately guarantee that not even one Israelite would be left behind (Exodus 6:1; 11:1; 12:29-42).

This narrative section sees the action through the eyes of the Egyptians. Set against the backdrop of firstborn death, the Israelites are told to go away! The Egyptian perspective offers no freedom songs or praises of deliverance. In the middle of the night, Moses and Aaron are ordered to take all their people, flocks, and herds and be gone.

Delivered

By God's hand, Moses and the Israelites were *delivered*. This account of the hasty departure from Egypt claims new life in the shadow of death. The Israelites fled from Egypt to precious freedom. No longer slaves, they were freed to serve God (Exodus 13:17-22). Freedom for Israel meant freedom for others—for the sake of the whole world.

These leave-taking steps of the Israelites were at God's leading and through the wilderness by God's own choosing. God's way strategically turned away from known threat and was marked with a generous display of tangible assurance. God was present among the Israelites and responsive to them.

Nevertheless, Israel's history is checkered with crises of faith; times the people seemed to utterly forget the grace, favor, and strength of God. During a time of exile, we hear in the psalms the cry of despair and the petition for deliverance. The anguish, doubt, and sheer terror of the psalmist are nearly palpable. Though comforted by the historical story, grief and sorrow still consume (Psalm 22:1-11).

From what does the psalmist need to be *delivered*? Physical illness, mental distress, faltering belief, enemy attack, imminent death? Complaints are rendered against God, other people, and even self.

Can the traditions of the past deliver assurance and trust? When the great compassion and holy love of God are starkly contrasted with the psalmist's own powerlessness, can the witness of the Israelites be enough to save?

Delivered
Read Exodus 13:17-22. What are the fundamental steps of deliverance illustrated by this move?

Compare the leave-taking of the Israelites to either the emancipation of slaves or a more contemporary image of deliverance.

Read Psalm 22:1-11. What movement is built into the psalmist's experience of deliverance? Think about ways in which chronicled history and witness might bring comfort and release to the forsaken in our world. Have any kind of survival or success stories in your own family inspired you to persevere? Tell about that history.

Look Closer
Using a Bible commentary, dig deeper into the logistics of this departure. See also Numbers 1–2. What would it take to notify and organize 2 million people (with flocks, herds, and plunder from the Egyptians) to pack their stuff and get ready to move out the next day? How long would it take to travel on foot, just to the next place (at least twenty-five miles)? Where did they go? Where did Pharaoh's army catch up with them? How does this level of detail affect your appreciation for what God actually accomplished with the people?

Deployed
Read Matthew 10:1-15. What were the disciples asked to do? How were they equipped to be deployed? Compare this example of deployment with present-day, customer-based, strategic sales, and field-office staffing models.

Read Genesis 46:1-7. How was Jacob blessed by his deployment to Egypt? We know this mostly in retrospect. How do we gain the discernment and the trust to recognize or to anticipate God's blessing in the midst of or as the result of plans that seem to go badly awry?

Remember the childhood game "Mother May I?" "Mother" stands a distance from the rest of the players. The players describe their desire to take steps to move toward "Mother" and ask "Mother, May I?" "Mother's" response is limited to either "Yes, you may" or "No, you may not." This playground deployment game depends on the whim and whimsy of "Mother." Describe a more faithful deployment model.

If you are in a mood to be playful, play this game for a few minutes. Encourage "Mother" to be as whimsical as "she" wishes. Then debrief the game, asking for feelings and impressions as persons were allowed or prevented from moving ahead.

Deployed

Jesus *deployed* the disciples for an urgent ministry to the house of Israel (Matthew 10:1-15). The itinerancy rules (verses 9-10) stripped them of the clutter of things that could jeopardize their authority. This simplification was not a knee-jerk reaction out of panic or necessity, but a statement of trust and reliance on God, just as Abram and Sarai went out bravely, not knowing.

The promises of God to the descendants of Abraham and Sarah are affirmed in this narrative (Genesis 46:1-7). The account describes the customary "God's call—human response—God's assurance" formula. God summoned, Jacob answered, God promised, and Jacob was *deployed* to take care of family business.

God took care of the past by authorizing Jacob to settle in Egypt. God sanctioned this move with an eye toward the future and blessings for years to come. God directed Jacob's every step.

FUSING THE WORD AND MY WORLD

Pick a leave-taking event from your life. Decide if it is best described by the word *displaced, delivered,* or *deployed.*

Fusing the Word and My World
In silence, individually rehearse your story. Identify the leave-taking events and circumstances in your life. Choose one. Were you *displaced, delivered,* or *deployed* by that move? Pick the word that best describes that action. How do you understand that word, based on your own experience?

32

Double Impact

Displaced, delivered, and *deployed* offer a way to characterize and sort leave-taking experiences. But, there are always at least two sides to every story. For example, the Israelites' response to Pharaoh's pursuing army in Exodus 14 (Exodus 14:8-14) demonstrates how a contradictory story-side can twist the way that leave-taking happens.

At least four pairs of dichotomous perspectives influence the Israelites' response to Pharaoh's army:

- faith vs. fear
- abide vs. flight
- trust vs. complain
- joy vs. regret

Any one of these contrary perspectives alone could effect leave-taking. But all four opposing forces seemed to close in on the Israelites as soon as the chasing chariots drew near. The momentum of the antagonists nearly shut down God's rescue operation. The Israelites knew more of Pharaoh's intent than of God's plan. The enemy was so near and God seemed so distant. Moses lifted up a vision of liberation and reclaimed God's power to deliver.

Double Impact
Identify some of the opposing forces that may have a potential impact on your own leave-taking. Go back to Susan's story, to one of the cases, or to your own experience to review these four pairs of responses to a leave-taking situation.

When have these forces closed in on you? Who helped you reclaim God's power to fight for you?

HEARD IN CONTEXT

The definition and understanding of the words *displaced, delivered,* and *deployed* rely on their context. The word *displaced* is interpreted by a chemist differently than by a refugee. The word *delivered* holds different meaning for the U.S. Postal Service, a local hospital, the grandchild of a slave, and a Jewish family commemorating the Passover. The word *deployed* means something different to a National Guard unit

SMALL GROUP

Heard in Context
Sit with one another. You may want to hear all the stories together, in "Break-Out" groups, or more privately. Tell about your leave-taking. Identify which word you chose to describe your experience. Talk about opposing forces. Seek to connect your *displaced, delivered,* or *deployed* experience with the God of Psalm 121.

than it does to a customer service-based repair business.

So far, *displaced*, *delivered*, and *deployed* have been defined and represented in contemporary culture, scriptural narrative, and personal experience. How are these words linked to faith? Recall your leave-taking event and the word you used to describe it. Now make the definition of that word relevant to a God who "will keep / your going out and your coming in / from this time on and forevermore" (Psalm 121:8). How do you interpret your word (*displaced, delivered,* or *deployed*) in this context?

GOING FORTH

The Exodus narrative calls the people of Israel from generation to generation to commemorate their deliverance from Pharaoh with the festivals of Passover and Unleavened Bread. Like these people of God, we also celebrate graduations, first jobs, marriages, births, new homes—the events of leave-taking in our lives.

There is both formal and informal ritual associated with sacred and secular comings and goings. A ritual becomes an expected part of a celebration in the life of a group. Cake at wedding receptions is a ritual food. Singing the "Star Spangled Banner" at athletic events is ritualistic. The ritual of gathering for worship includes the symbolic action of candle-lighting. Even going out to eat after church can be claimed as part of a Sunday morning ritual.

Formulate a leave-taking ritual together. Use it at the end of this and the rest of the following sessions to celebrate your life and journey together.

Going Forth

A leave-taking ritual may include Scripture, prayer, silent reflection or meditation, music, symbolic actions of belonging or signs of Christian love, and a blessing. Use one or more of the following elements for your ritual:

- Scripture: Psalm 22:4-5 (Confession of faith in God who liberates)

- Prayer: Prayers of thanksgiving that rehearse what God has done, past and present

- Blessing: Psalm 121:7-8

SHOW ME WILDERNESS

This session is designed to acknowledge the life-giving potential of a wilderness venture.

GETTING STARTED

Play the "Die Game." Role a die. Respond to the statement that corresponds with the number on the die.

1. Specify an image of God that holds meaning for you.

2. Tell about a song, phrase, or verse that describes daily living with God to you.

3. Characterize someone who has walked with you on your journey of faith.

4. Identify something about God's created/natural order that is truly awesome to you.

5. Explain your understanding of the phrase "daily bread."

6. Describe a time when you were on the receiving end of an intentional teaching or testing.

Getting Started
Greet one another. Welcome and identify any newcomers. Invite everyone to offer a brief, "life since we last met" update.

WILDERNESS FACES

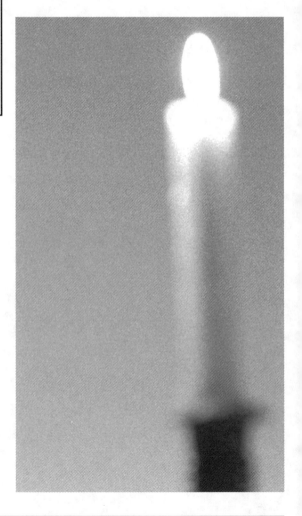

Wilderness Faces

Reflect on the texts in the Bible boxes in this session and how each portrays wilderness. You may choose to explore all the texts and live with the diverse and multifaceted wilderness faces, choose just one of the narratives, follow the trek of the Israelites, or use Break-Out groups to focus on one or more of the wilderness images.

Begin by keeping a time of quiet with the Scripture. Break the silence only with personal stories that parallel or affirm a face of wilderness.

Bible traditions claim the wilderness as a time of testing, teaching, and disciplining. Problems and complaints are characteristic of this death-filled context. But, so are the oases of God's concern and action. Wilderness crises connect God to ordinary, daily needs. God couples the power of nature and human wisdom to heal and give life. Through examples from both Old and New Testaments, we see how God faced the wilderness with persons of faith to see them through.

Dead-End Desert

Say the word *wilderness* and an image of barren desert pops into mind! *Desert* is almost synonymous with *wilderness*. The promises of a new thing, growth, and restoration offered by the prophet Isaiah reflect a dry, parched, and life-threatening wilderness land.

Enemies in hot pursuit, swirling sand, unquenchable thirst, and wild beasts—these are images of which nightmares are made—our nightmares! Use contemporary imagery to represent Isaiah's wilderness. Consider your own "drought conditions" and all that threatens your life.

On an Oasis

The Israelites were delivered from their bondage—handed over by Pharaoh to start their new life as the people of God. Moses, Aaron, Miriam, and the people of Israel began their new life with God, the giver of life. Together they embarked on a venture of faithful living in the betwixt and between wilderness, from oasis to oasis (Exodus 15:22–16:16).

The Exodus account of Israel's departure from Egypt included men, women, and children—Israelites and others. In your mind's eye, imagine the scene as Moses ordered Israel out from the Red Sea. Put yourself into the face of this wilderness.

**Dead-End Desert
Read Isaiah 43:16-21
and Isaiah 44:3-5.**

Examine the empty, dead, and hopeless details of this wilderness face. What do prophetic promises of ways, water, and willows tell you about this wilderness wasteland?

For some, the starkness of urban living, for example, may seem a more familiar image of wilderness. What contemporary image of wilderness do you hold? What makes it so?

**On an Oasis
Read Exodus 15:22–
16:16** silently once. Then, read it again.

Look for sounds, smells, sights, touches, and even tastes. Hear the complaining. Smell the brackish water. See the wide, barren desert. Feel the movement of the crowd. Taste the sweet manna. Make a list of sounds, smells, sights, touches, and tastes.

Read the narrative again, silently. This time, begin to think of how you feel about the deprivation and extremely harsh and miserable conditions of the Exodus wilderness. Is the wilderness a surprise? God's promise unfulfilled? a test? a lesson?

Flee and Fly

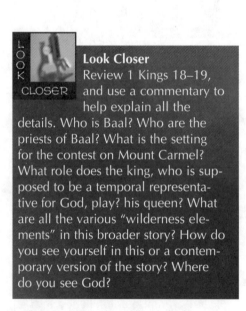

Flee and Fly
Read I Kings 19:1-13a. Here Elijah is portrayed as a very zealous man. He looked for God in his wilderness. How did expecting God shape the face of Elijah's wilderness?

Rate your wilderness experience along a continuum between "god-forsaken" and "God-filled." Where does your wilderness fall along this line? How closely do you look for God? How do you recognize God who can come in many ways (such as earthquake, fire, and silence)?

Now move forward a few centuries. A zealous Elijah has killed the prophets of Baal, the god of rain and vegetation. The victory was God's! The drought ended. News of the stabbing deaths has reached Queen Jezebel. She threatened Elijah's life and he fled (1 Kings 18–19).

Elijah went a day's journey into the wilderness. Tired of looking over his shoulder, he sat down. Even after participating in such a spectacular victory for God, he was burned-out and depressed. In despair (and perhaps a large measure of self-pity and "awful-izing"), Elijah sought death in the godforsaken wilderness.

It would make good sense to seek death in the wilderness, wouldn't it? But God is in Elijah's wilderness. Elijah's wilderness is not godforsaken or beyond redemption. This wilderness is a God-filled resting place and refuge of hope (19:4-9).

Look Closer
Review 1 Kings 18–19, and use a commentary to help explain all the details. Who is Baal? Who are the priests of Baal? What is the setting for the contest on Mount Carmel? What role does the king, who is supposed to be a temporal representative for God, play? his queen? What are all the various "wilderness elements" in this broader story? How do you see yourself in this or a contemporary version of the story? Where do you see God?

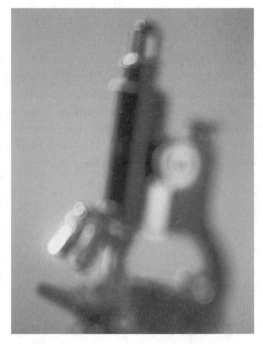

Dare to Dust

Fast forward again several centuries and we see in the early verses of Matthew 10 that Jesus deployed his twelve disciples for ministry. They traveled light and stayed where they were welcomed. If not welcomed, they were trained to "shake off the dust" from their feet (10:14) and leave town.

The disciples would "shake off the dust" to keep themselves clean and holy. We dust when we clean our living space and vehicles. Sometimes we deep clean to make space for something new.

Wilderness can be a time for "shaking off the dust." This wilderness face gives permission to jar loose bad habits, blow off unnecessary or unsolicited responsibilities, or clear away the cobwebs and make room for a new reality.

Dare to Dust
Read Matthew 10:5-14. What are the specific instructions? It seems that Jesus wants the disciples to do and accomplish quite a lot with very few comforts or resources. What do you make of that? What resources do you need to do what God wills for you?

If they were not welcome, the disciples would "shake off the dust" and move on to the next house or the next town. When have you dared to dust in your wilderness? What did you shake off, jar loose, blow off, and clear away? What new reality had space to grow in your "clean house"? How do you know the difference between when God wants you to move and when you move because of your own disappointment, disenchantment, or disgust?

Look Closer
Use a Bible dictionary to look up *hospitality* for further insight into why the disciples could reasonably expect to be offered food and a place to stay without payment.

Impatient Initiative

Beginning something new, though, can take a while to get started. As the history of God's people who would become Israel began, God promised to make Abram a great nation, to make his name great, and to bless him. Abram abandoned his own homeland for the unknown place God sent him and relinquished his own ancestral bonds in faithful response to these promises (Genesis 12:1-9).

Impatient Initiative
Read Genesis 16:1-16.
Focus on the actions and initiative of Abram and Sarai. Pay particular attention to their determination and competent planning. What actions are symptomatic of their "defective" wilderness faith?

Once in the wilderness, the promises made to Abram and Sarai were delayed. The great sorrow and disgrace of Sarai's barrenness provided fertile ground for impatient human initiative. Fueled by this impatience, Abram and Sarai found a way to force the promise of God by their own actions. The face of their wilderness turned ugly as they began to trust the work of their own hands rather than to wait for God (Genesis 16:1-16).

SIT WITH THE WORD

We have always had trouble trusting in the word of God. The crowds in Jesus' "headquarters" of Capernaum seemed more interested in filling their stomachs than in seeking God. They claimed they needed signs of God in order to make their way. While the miracle of the loaves and fishes did capture their attention, the crowds just ate the bread and missed the point (John 6:1-15; 22-59).

The Capernaum crowd had no concept of the bread of heaven of which Jesus spoke. They never asked Jesus to explain it—they just knew they wanted it. What's your take on this? Was the crowd reacting to the possibility of a never-ending food supply, or did they truly recognize their own spiritual hunger?

Their wilderness was spiritual and Jesus offered them the food of believers. They do their own doubting and murmuring—just like those Israelites clamoring for water and food between oases centuries before. Jesus gave himself as the gift of God's abiding presence for all times. And, like their ancient ancestors, some of them believed and understood, and others didn't, including the disciples.

FUSING THE WORD AND MY WORLD

Hoy

Hoy has a secret. When she was a young teen, Hoy was involved in something that she knew was wrong and truly believes that God will punish her. So for years, she has wandered away from God and tried to make it on her own. Hoy's secret, and her guilt, have forced her into isolation. She's put her very life at risk.

Even though Hoy is not physically wandering in a literal desert, she is in the wilderness. Hoy has strayed from God's power—the power to bless, love, and offer life, even in the face of death.

Fusing the Word and My World

Hoy
One person should begin telling the story of Hoy, beginning with one or two sentences beyond the very brief introduction here. Then the next person should pick up the story and add details until everyone who wants to has contributed. (You can leave the story open-ended.) What is Hoy's secret? What are the characteristics of her wilderness? What might she do next?

CALL TO COMFORT

God's people need comforting! Comfort turns suffering away. Comforting requires active intervention and help.

God turns to the chosen ones in forgiveness—whatever was is now over. Forgiveness is tightly bound to the deliverance promised by the cry for comfort (Isaiah 40:1-5).

The call to comfort is heard and a voice cries out. A highway in the wilderness is promised—a new way where only insurmountable and impassable obstacles just stood.

Call to Comfort
Read Isaiah 40:1-5.
What does Hoy need to be comforted? What might you do to help prepare a way for God's loving power in Hoy's life?

THREE VOICES IN THE WILDERNESS

Three Voices in the Wilderness
When have you known the betwixt and between wilderness? What is it like where you wander?

Answer Lee out of your own wilderness experience. What wilderness comfort have you known? How do you explain the way of comfort prepared for you? Can you claim that there is God-given life, even in the wilderness?

Amanda: Explain wilderness comfort? OK. It's all wrapped up in God's power to love and forgive. God's awesome power brings life, even in the middle of a death-filled wilderness.

Lee: Great—a slick and ready Sunday school answer! So, someone like Hoy runs from God into the wilderness, rounds the next curve, and finds evidence of a loving, healing, and life-giving God at the next intersection? So, what does she do? Everything is just fine then?

Cheslav: Yes, it's a miracle of the wilderness. The wilderness of the Israelites was dry. They were thirsty. They complained. God and Moses figured out a way to provide drinking water so they would not die. God's got a wilderness side. This water comforted and gave life—not like the water that drowned the Egyptians at the Red Sea.

Amanda: So, the rain that produced the manna when the Israelites were hungry is also a miracle of the wilderness. These storm clouds comforted—not like the clouds that made the hail that destroyed the Egyptian food supply.

Lee: So, what do I see of that miracle in my wilderness? How do I know the difference between the rain that brings manna and the rain that brings hail, the water that quenches thirst and the water that drowns me? How do I get a way of comfort prepared for me in my wilderness?

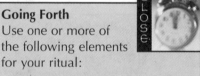
Going Forth
CLOSE
Use one or more of the following elements for your ritual:

- Scripture: Isaiah 35:1-10 (Signs of abundant life in the wilderness)

- Prayer: Silent prayers and specific prayers of petition for life-giving ways, even in the wilderness

- Blessing: Numbers 6:24-26

GOING FORTH

Make use of the leave-taking ritual developed with your group at the end of Session 2.

TESTING 1-2-3

> This session is designed to present wilderness testing as a chance to influence personal identity.

GETTING STARTED

Complaining and whining are just part of being human. The comic page is a great place to explore human nature. Look for complaining and whining in a week's worth of funny papers. Check it out: Who is whining? What about? Is there any response to the complaining?

Getting Started

Greet one another. Welcome and identify any new-comers. Invite one another to offer a brief, "life since we last met" update.

For this session, use a "Virginia Reel" method of dialogue. Divide the group in two. Each group will line up, either in random order or according to some formula, such as oldest to youngest. Lines will face each other and pair off. Pairs will change by having one line move one person to the left. When discussing the issues, do not try to force consensus or to reconcile differing perspectives between partners.

WILDERNESS TROUBLE

Wilderness Trouble
Read Exodus 17:1-7,
and spend about three
minutes considering
each of the following three questions. After each question, change partners.

1. What was the cause of the wilderness trouble in this episode?
2. How did the people respond to the trouble?
3. How did the people experience God's creative action?

Follow the same process for Numbers 11:1-35. Then shift again and compare the two accounts. Focus particularly on the people's complaints, Moses' role, and God's response.

God had freed, led, and provided for the Israelites. Now we meet them out in the wilderness stuck somewhere on the way from God's promise to its fulfillment (Exodus 17:1-7). Being led by God does not necessarily mean taking the most direct route to the next oasis. The chaos of life on the move in the wilderness was starting to take its toll. Patience and trust were wearing thin.

Later, after the covenant at Sinai (Exodus 19–24) and in the shadow of the "golden calf" incident (Exodus 32), the murmuring of the Israelites turned the corner and became—whining!

The people grumbled so much about their hunger that God sent them more than they could possibly eat (Numbers 11:1-35). But God was angry: "You shall eat . . . for a whole month—until it comes out your nostrils and becomes loathsome to you—because you have rejected the LORD" (11:19-20). Then the quails came, and the people gathered at least ten homers (six bushels, but perhaps as many as fourteen). And then came the plague; so bad that the place was called Kibroth-hattaavah, "Graves of craving."

VOICES FROM THE WILDERNESS

After reading the Scriptures about the Israelites' hardships and complaints in the wilderness, Shayla, Jerrod, and Nicole venture their own opinions.

Shayla: Maybe the wilderness isn't so godforsaken after all. There seems to be so much cosmic potential out there.

Jerrod: *If* the Israelites are thirsty, *then* God gives water. *If* they are hungry, *then* God gives food. *If* the chosen ones push God over the edge, *then* God really unleashes the cosmic powers!

Nicole: I'd say that surviving the fire of God's anger would be a defining moment for anybody.

Shayla: They set up God! Their griping was just plain unfaithful. How much proof did the Israelites need? God delivered them, made promises, and cared for them. All they had to do was be obedient, and all they did was complain. They asked for God's anger!

Nicole: So, as long as we are obedient and faithful, we will be OK? If you have enough faith, then God will act to fix whatever is wrong?

Wilderness Voices
Keeping in mind the discussion about the wilderness complaints, how would you answer Shayla? If the wilderness is not godforsaken, was it any less dangerous when God punished Israel for griping?

How would you answer Nicole? Is faith enough for a life of smooth growth? Is that what "OK" means?

How do you hear Jerrod's "if-then" statements?—as a witness to the awesome grace and power of God, as an attempt to force and limit God's hand, or as something else? Explain.

Biblical Studies 101: The Wilderness

The wilderness is a desolate wasteland. The Hebrew *midbar* describes an uninhabited, parched, and dangerous place. It is inhospitable—incapable of supporting human life.

Topographically, wilderness may be poor steppeland surrounding an oasis or marginally tillable pasture land with thickets and brushwood. It may be true desert without trees or vegetation, barren and void of flocks or herdsmen.

To be in the wilderness is to be cut off from life. Wilderness is synonymous with utter darkness, destitution, and abandonment.

For Jesus, the wilderness was a time and place of preparation, a rite of passage toward public ministry. Jesus was endangered by hunger, thirst, and a demonic character. At risk was the realization of Jesus' mission. Satan offered a shortcut—the chance to use miracle, mystery, and power to compel belief. Jesus forfeited this coercive authority and refused the charade.

SIT WITH THE WORD

**Sit With the Word
Read Luke 4:1-13.**
What are the three temptations? What was Jesus' response to them? What resources did he have at his command? How did the decisions made in the face of these three temptations define Jesus' identity? How did they inform Jesus' ministry?

When you think about your own temptations, how many of them are life threatening, either in the short or long term? How do you address your own temptations? What resources are at your command? Does your faith ever make any difference? Explain.

How do you understand your own dependence, faithfulness, and trust when confronted by temptation? Luke 4:13 says that the devil departed until "an opportune time." What did that mean for Jesus? What does it mean for you?

The wilderness is a testing ground for faith. Commentaries claim that the testing and discipline of the wilderness is like the instruction or teaching of a loving parent. Jesus' wilderness test presented him with temptations for greatness—greatness according to human standards.

The first of the temptations (Luke 4:3-4) tested personal *dependence*. Jesus had his own power. Stones to bread could have been Jesus' first miracle—a sure sign of his greatness. We are tempted when we have a chance to get what we want and to meet our own needs. But, the faithful standard for success is to put ourselves out of the way and let God be God. While it is our nature to try to make it under our own power and on our own, it is the disposition of God to provide for us.

Faithfulness was the second test (Luke 4:5-8). Jesus was offered the world. He could have been the political messiah—the great king that everyone expected. When we are offered the world on a string we are tempted by the chance to have it all and to get our own way. Jesus could not submit to this world's rules for success and definitions of greatness. Faithful journeying through the wilderness is measured by an unwavering eagerness to worship and give way to God's way.

The last scene (Luke 4:9-12) tested *trust*. The evil one dared Jesus to coerce faith in God. Jesus was challenged to hail the angel's attention, take a flying leap, and survive—all to force God's hand and to show off God's power. When we boldly try to tell God how to be God instead of trusting God to be God, we try to limit God's greatness. The source of Jesus' success is in the power of the Spirit. Our capacity to resist temptation is gauged by our faithful ability to claim this power. A faithful wilderness experience trusts God to be God, to hear our cries, and to act out of steadfast love.

As a writer, Luke develops this whole scene in great anticipation of the onset of Jesus' ministry. This journey and his experience in the wilderness just adds to the significance of Jesus' arrival in Galilee.

Jennifer

Jennifer was home for a long weekend to put the finishing touches on early summer wedding plans. One afternoon she got back to the house in time for supper and heard unusual sounds from the family room downstairs. Her stepfather had just come home from work and retired to the lower-level family room with a drink. A few minutes later, Jennifer heard more strange sounds and went downstairs to see what was going on. Jennifer's stepfather raped her.

Thrust into the wilderness by something beyond her control, Jennifer plowed her way through the wilderness by asking, "Why me?"

CASE STUDY

Jennifer
What temptations are found in the face of "Why me?" "Why here?" "Why now?" questions? Imagine Jennifer's trauma. What might she do? How might she feel? Does Jennifer deal with this on her own, plot revenge, or turn to God?

Perhaps you have asked the "Why" questions or you know someone who has. How unreasonable is it to think that God might use times of distress as a means toward a fuller understanding of who we were created to be? How reasonable is it to patiently trust God? Explain.

Consider the difference between a "Why me?" response and a "What now?" response. What is the difference? What difference might it make?

FUSING THE WORD AND MY WORLD

Fusing the Word and My World
Review this summary of wilderness feelings and experiences. Close your eyes and concentrate for several minutes on this observation: "Their faith only went as far as they could see—it forgot the past and was afraid of the future." How well does this summarize your experience? Are you long on control and short on patience? What message is there here for you in terms of dealing with your own wilderness experiences and feelings?

What does it mean to you to think that in God, your future will be secure?

Read Psalm 40:1-3. Write your own version, using metaphors of your own choosing for such images as "miry bog," and "set my feet upon a rock." Could this be your psalm? Does it convey a sense of faith, hope, and security? Explain.

Being committed to Christ does not exempt us from brokenness in our day-to-day life. We live with everything from personal pain to worldwide suffering. We react to wilderness times (even while in the same wilderness) in distinct and varied ways.

The Israelites operated in the wilderness out of fear. They feared for themselves and for their future. Their faith only went as far as they could see—it forgot the past and was afraid of the future. In spite of being called God's chosen, they tested both God and faith on a case-by-case basis.

Jesus remembered the Israelite story of the wilderness and believed that his future would be secure. He was patient and trusting, even at personal risk. As God's Beloved, it was as if the temptations were some sort of weird gift. Jesus could have short-circuited the system or taken the easy way out. Instead, he used the work of the evil one to help see himself more clearly.

Somewhere between the wilderness of the Israelites and Jesus' temptation, a psalmist reports deliverance from death-threatening trouble. Read Psalm 40:1-3. Listen to the anxious and prayerful yearning for God's help. God delivered and restored this one's life, according to God's own wisdom and time.

The psalmist's praise gives witness to the limitless power of God. This new song is a significant offering to others—a chance to see and fear in the face of God's power. This is an awestruck fear that reverently praises God's power; a wonderful, trembling fear that can claim complete trust in God's saving grace and love.

VOICES STILL
IN THE WILDERNESS

Jerrod: Enough faith? I'm not sure that trying to measure the quantity of faith, like water in a cup, is quite right. Sure the Israelites may have been down a quart or two in the faith department; but Jesus?

Shayla: Jesus had to have had enough faith. But, his wilderness pain was no less painful and his uncertainty was no more certain.

Jerrod: Jesus got through to the other side of wilderness without forcing God's power. Jesus trusted God's power—that's quality, not quantity. Jesus patiently waited out his time in the wilderness with Satan.

Nicole: The psalmist waited patiently, too! No anxious or panic-stricken fear here. This is a clear-cut case of complete trust in God.

Shayla: What does that kind of quality faith look like to you and me and people like Jennifer who are caught in evil with no warning and no protection? How do I get that kind of patient and trusting faith? What's in it for me?

Voices Still in the Wilderness Jerrod responds to Nicole's comment in the first conversation about "having enough faith." What does that mean? Is faith quantifiable? Do you have to have a certain amount before God listens to your prayers, for example? Explain.

What does it mean to describe faith in terms of quality and quantity? Answer Shayla's question about quality faith in light of Jennifer's wilderness situation. What might a patient and trusting faith look like to Jennifer?

Think about your own wilderness experience, or that of someone else you know. Was wilderness lived more in fearful, restless anxiety or more in patient trust?

PATIENT PRACTICES

Jesus relied on the power of the Holy Spirit, solitude, fasting, the witness of Scripture, and prayer to patiently wait out Satan in the wilderness. The Spirit of God provided the energy to sustain Jesus' patient waiting and his capacity to trust in the promises of joyful and abundant life.

All that Jesus did in the wilderness was for God. Solitude offered the space he needed to wait quietly and expectantly *for* God. Fasting relieved distractions and made "heart-room" *for* God. Scripture supported his efforts to listen *for* God. Prayer hoped *for* God to act.

Patient Practices Answer Shayla's second question for yourself. How do you get Jesus' kind of patient and trusting wilderness faith?

I.D. Me
Sit with another person. In the same spirit as the psalmist, risk sharing your story in the hope that others might be strengthened.

Claim the defining value of such experiences—what's in it for you? Who are you because of (or, in spite of) your wilderness experience?

Measure the quality of your wilderness faith by degrees of patience and trust. Identify what you still need from God to strengthen your patient and trusting faith for life in the wilderness.

I.D. ME!

This quality combination of patient practices made trust possible for Jesus. But, patient trust is tough! You have to look for the "big picture," claim that you are worth the effort, and stick-to-it for the long haul.

From the wilderness, Jesus returned to Galilee with a deeper understanding of self-identity, purpose, and worth. Entertain the possibility that patient trust in the thick of your own wilderness might do the same for you.

GOING FORTH

Make use of the leave-taking ritual developed with your group at the end of Session 2.

Going Forth
Use one or more of the following elements for your ritual:

- Scripture: 1 Peter 1:3-7 (Affirmation of the hope that comes in the midst of wilderness living)
- Prayer: Silent prayer and specific prayers of petition and intercession
- Blessing: Deuteronomy 28:6

Session 5

CHOSEN AS GOD'S OWN

> This session is designed to offer an identity as chosen and treasured possessions of God.

GETTING STARTED

Think about your most treasured possession. Take turns telling about the one thing you would pick up and take with you if your home ever caught fire. Be as specific as possible about its value to you.

Getting Started
Greet one another. Welcome and identify any newcomers. Invite one another to offer a brief, "life since we last met" update.

CHOSEN AND TREASURED

After more than two months of Exodus wilderness wandering and testing, Moses and the Israelites camped at Sinai, in front of the sacred mountain. God chose the people of Israel to be the holy people of God (Exodus 19:1-8).

Chosen and Treasured
Read Exodus 19:1-8.
Silently reflect and engage in this guided meditation.

SMALL GROUP

Guided meditation offers an opportunity to get involved with the life and situations of someone else. In this case, it may lead you to discover something more about yourself and our God.

The leader will use the descriptive narrative provided to set the stage and give other group members time for thought and reflection. Silence and time are both important for a meditative experience. The meditation must be read slowly, phrase by phrase, to allow plenty of time for listening, contemplation, reflection, and response.

What did you feel and sense during the meditation about the destruction and desolation of the tornado? about losing everything precious, including your "treasure"? How did it feel to find that special something? Can you make the leap to sense how it feels to be a treasured "possession" of God? Have you ever thought of yourself that way before? Do you believe it?

Use the questions that follow the meditation to focus discussion on the experience of Israel as a covenant people. What does that mean?

Relax in a comfortable sitting position. Close your eyes. Take a couple of deep breaths. Imagine for a moment that you've just survived a classic level three or four tornado. You, the people, and the pets you care about are all scared, but safe.

Imagine coming up the basement stairs and finding nothing. Absolutely nothing. Look around—there is a tangled mess of debris, but nothing that resembles home. There is no evidence of vegetation or trees, no lawn chairs or out buildings; no car, no doghouse. Nothing that used to be still is. Everything in the house, including the house, is gone—scattered to the wind— gone.

You begin to dig through what's left, looking for your most treasured possession. What is it? Maybe it's a favorite CD, a work of art, a photo album, a book or letter, a musical instrument, a diary or journal, a childhood memento, something that's been in the family for years. Look for it.

It's nowhere to be found. Sit for a minute with the memory of this treasured possession. What does it mean to you? How is it important to you?

Time passes. Cleanup is over and life resumes. Rebuilding begins, and at least a few neighbors are back in their homes. Lost and found ads begin to appear in the local newspaper. Individual household items have been found scattered across the countryside, some many, many miles away. Local city officials provide a place to gather these items and a chance for people like you to come look. One day you go, just to look; and there it is! You pick it up and hold it in your hand—your treasured possession.

You too are a treasured possession— God's treasured possession. God seeks you, bears you up on eagles' wings, brings you to

God's self, and loves and cares for you.
Imagine that!

Rest on the spirit of this awesome claim
for your life; and when you are ready, qui-
etly come back to this place and open your
eyes.

The people of Israel were God's treasured
possession . . . "a royal priesthood, a holy
nation"—a people set apart as God's chosen
(1 Peter 2:9-10). The Israelites had status,
an identity, and a purpose. They were val-
ued. They were expected to BE God's people in the world. How did they live up to
this claim? How do you live up to this
claim?

SIT WITH THE WORD

Chosen Israelites

Motivated out of love, grace, and
promise, God acted. God chose the Israelites
to be dedicated totally to God. God set them
apart as holy to serve and make real God's
ways in the world. The Israelites possessed
no particular attributes or special qualifica-
tions. They were not the greatest among the
nations, but rather the least and the fewest.
God "set his love on" the children of
Abraham (Deuteronomy 7:6-13). The rela-

tionship is grounded in loving
and keeping.

God is the keeper of the
covenant. Disobedience and
unfaithfulness hinder God's
work. Dealing with that is a
matter for God—justice, tem-
pered with mercy, forgiveness,
and compassion. The people
are called to mirror God's way
with them to the world.

> **Sit With the Word**
> Explore the Scripture
> texts to discover how
> each passage character-
> izes the "holy" people. You may
> choose to explore all the texts,
> choose just one of the narratives,
> focus on the chosen Israelites, or use
> "Break-Out" groups to connect to
> each one of the passages.

Chosen Servant

The words of the prophet describe both an individual and a faith community (Isaiah 42:1-9). These verses are often read with Jesus' baptismal accounts to affirm his identity as the Son of God. This same "Servant Song" also speaks clearly to the role of Israel as God's light to the nations.

The designation of *servant*, to be one out of many, was a public action of God. The servant was chosen and equipped for a specific task. The servant worked with a patient and gentle spirit. Quietly, without clamor or cries, the servant took care not to further wound the weak and fragile.

This servant is a prototype of all that love God—an instrument chosen to bring about justice in the world.

Chosen and Holy Fellowship

These brief verses (1 Peter 2:9-10) tell how to do and be church. Out of darkness, insignificance, and reprisal, the church was transformed by God's unexpected grace to a new reality of light and love.

The church was compelled by the privilege of its relationship to God and its obligations to one another. This belonging is the God-standard for faith communities. How does your local congregation measure up?

Read from these "chosen" Scriptures:
■ Deuteronomy 7:6-13
■ Isaiah 42:1-9
■ 1 Peter 2:9-10
■ Matthew 9:35–10:8

Ask the following questions of these "chosen" texts:
■ What were the expectations of the chosen?
■ How was the relationship with the chosen ratified?
■ How were the expectations fostered?
■ How was the relationship nurtured?

Use a commentary to help answer the questions. Summarize and interpret these "chosen" texts to other group members. Compare the expectations and the impact of the relationship on the chosen.

Chosen Apostles

Against a mixed backdrop of growing popularity, expanding ministry, and intensifying opposition, Jesus chose twelve apostles. These ordinary men were chosen, equipped, and sent out as representatives of Jesus (Matthew 9:35–10:8). They were ordinary, but their work was extraordinary: to "cure the sick, raise the dead, cleanse the lepers, cast out demons" (10:8).

If this command follows literally for all those who are called to a life of discipleship, we have an incredible task. It was believed to be entirely possible two thousand years ago; we probably scoff at it now: Raise the dead? Cleanse lepers? Really! But the Book of Acts is full of examples of the disciples having such power and the faith to work that power. Is that power and level of faith lost on the "ordinary" Christian these days? Does our incredulity at the prospect of doing what seem to be miracles limit the spiritual power we have at our command? Are we chosen, but for lesser work? No. We are among God's beloved.

Recall times when you have been chosen. Get beyond the pickup, playground ballgames. Center on a meaning-filled circumstance when you were chosen by another for a significant role, position, or task.

- Against what standards was the decision made?
- How were you assessed?
- What did the one doing the choosing expect of you?
- How were/are those expectations fostered?
- Characterize your relationship with the one who chose you.
- How was your value or worth influenced by being chosen?

Relate your experience of being chosen with the cases in the "chosen" Scriptures.

FUSING THE WORD AND MY WORLD

A Beloved Identity

Matthew's account of Jesus' baptism reports that a voice from heaven (God's voice) is heard to say, "This is my Son, the Beloved, with whom I am well pleased" (Matthew 3:17). In that moment was a surge of certainty and self-understanding for Jesus. God willed Jesus' identity as the Son of God at his baptism, an identity that was radically different and greater than John the Baptist. At his baptism, Jesus is who God says he is. Matthew, Mark, and

Fusing the Word and My World

A Beloved Identity
Read the account of Jesus' baptism (Matthew 3:13-16) and the commentary. Have you ever thought about your own baptism as an identity-making event? What does that mean to you to be a beloved child of God?

Luke all report that immediately after this announcement came a powerful wilderness experience, the Temptation, for Jesus. His own self-identity and identity as God's Beloved were tested immediately.

Can believers, now some two thousand years later, hear these words in the context of our own baptism? Imagine God's voice from heaven heard at your own baptism— "This my daughter, the beloved, with you I am well pleased," or "This is my son, the beloved, with you I am well pleased." This is the voice that boldly proclaims love for you in the face of a wilderness full of other voices that dare you to do something spectacular to prove that you are worth loving.

How does your baptism make a difference? It establishes your identity as the beloved and an heir of God's promises (Galatians 3:26-29). At your baptism, you are who God says you are!

Valerie

I went to the hospital as soon as I heard. Valerie had been hit head-on by a drunk driver. Her condition was serious.

Valerie and I had grown up in the same little town, neighborhood, and church. But by high school, we had really gone our separate ways. Now we are nearly a dozen years and a thousand miles from home, and we are working for the same company.

By the time I got to the hospital, several medical professionals were hastily attending to Valerie. She was stable, but drifting in and out of consciousness. Valerie kept mumbling something each time she would wake, and each time the doctors and nurses would work to quiet her.

The flurry of activity around Valerie started to slow, and I tried hard to listen. "Don't forget!" Valerie said it over and over

Valerie
Apparently, Valerie knew down deep that she was a child of God. What difference can a strong sense of identity make in a crisis? What difference might Valerie's identity as a child of God make during her recovery? What witness might it have made to the friend keeping vigil at the hospital?

Some people identify who they are by family name (or clan or tribe or nationality) and tradition. The actions of any one family member often reflect the name by which they are known. When has your identity as a member of your family of origin made a difference in your actions?

Exodus: Leaving Behind, Moving On

and over again. I thought maybe she was trying to keep some details of the accident together in her head.

Finally, I asked, "Don't forget what Valerie?"

Out of her mouth came dozen-year-old words that we had heard a thousand times—the same words spoken by our pastor when she was baptized and we were confirmed—"Don't forget! No matter what, you are a child of God."

Look Closer
Baptized Christians are known as beloved. Imagine that your actions reflect the name of Beloved. When could just "knowing who you are" make a difference in your wilderness?

Baptism is truly an identifying moment in the life of a Christian. You may actually be able to remember the day of your baptism or can recall stories told over the years about the day of your baptism.

Gather good china cups and a pitcher of water to help remember and claim the actions and promises of God made at your baptism.

Sit in a circle. Pass out cups and fill each one with water. Hold the cup and touch the water. Quietly imagine a baptismal scene. Envision God's loving Spirit being poured over you.

In turn, each participant will face the person to the left, and ask, "By what name are you known?" The respondent will answer by speaking his or her first, middle (maiden

or former), and last names. The participant will sprinkle the respondent with a little water and all group members will respond by saying, "This is my [daughter/son, N. _____], the Beloved. Remember your baptism and be thankful."

Turn to the baptism ritual in your hymnal or book of worship. What are the questions asked of the person to be baptized or of the sponsors? What vows are made? What is the intended effect of these commitments? Have your vows or the vows made for you been kept? What do they mean to you as an adult?

Chosen as God's Own

Becoming Beloved

SMALL GROUP

Becoming Beloved
What are the "social consequences" of being beloved? How do you move between the high ideal of being the beloved and becoming the beloved? How do you start to "close the gap"?

Talk together about how to claim this identity. Share practical ways to bridge being the beloved and becoming the beloved in all that you think, say, and do every day. Specifically describe what you still need to realize your beloved identity in open and obvious ways.

According to Henri Nouwen, we spend our life claiming our identity and *becoming* the Beloved. In *Life of the Beloved*, he says, "Becoming the Beloved means letting the truth of our Belovedness become enfleshed in everything we think, say or do."

He goes on to ask how one struggles to "close the gap that exists between what [you] know [your]self to be and the countless specific realities of everyday life."

CLOSE

Going Forth
Use one or more of the following elements for your ritual:

- Scripture: Isaiah 42:1-9 (Identity as God's chosen, the beloved)

- Prayer: Prayers that challenge and support one another to become the Beloved and to live a life that reflects the love, justice, mercy, and compassion of God

- Blessing: Romans 15:13

GOING FORTH

Make use of the leave-taking ritual developed with your group at the end of Session 2.

OOPS! WRONG TURN

This session is designed to identify influences that delay exodus arrival or lead to the wrong destination and to regain perspective on a more faithful journey.

GETTING STARTED

We are chosen ones, known before we are born, and treasured possessions of God. We are called "Beloved" and so we are. God promises to be our God. But everyday *places* and *things* demand our attention, other *voices* shout loudly and things go awry. Other *forces* take the place of God.

What *places*, *things*, *voices*, and *forces* can take the place of God in our lives?

Getting Started

Greet one another. Welcome and identify any newcomers.
Invite one another to offer a brief, "life since we last met" update.

Create an 8" x 5" nameplate by folding a full sheet of paper in half. Print your name boldly on one side of the fold. On the other side, designate four quadrants. Using words or symbols, answer these questions, starting in the top left corner and working clockwise.

- If places were to be substituted for God, what might that look like?
- If things were to be substituted for God, what might that look like?
- If voices were to be substituted for God, what might that look like?
- If forces were to be substituted for God, what might that look like?

Briefly compare answers to each of the four questions, and record on your nameplate answers held in common with other group members. What does this tell you about some of the places, things, voices, and forces that take the place of God in our lives?

INSTEAD OF GOD?

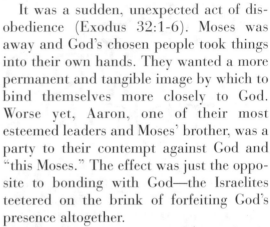

B
I
B
L
E

Instead of God?
Read Exodus 32:1-6.
What is the nature of the Israelites' sin? Why was it sin? What prompted it, and who participated? What excuse might they have had? Is it possible that they did not know they were engaged in something that was sinful, or at least inappropriate?

Aaron was a leader, second only to Moses; but he was in the thick of things. What reasons or pressures might have prompted his actions? What happened to him as a result?

It was a sudden, unexpected act of disobedience (Exodus 32:1-6). Moses was away and God's chosen people took things into their own hands. They wanted a more permanent and tangible image by which to bind themselves more closely to God. Worse yet, Aaron, one of their most esteemed leaders and Moses' brother, was a party to their contempt against God and "this Moses." The effect was just the opposite to bonding with God—the Israelites teetered on the brink of forfeiting God's presence altogether.

Pay attention to the *places*, *things*, *voices*, and *forces* that threaten to take the place of God in this narrative. God promised to be their God—to lead them to

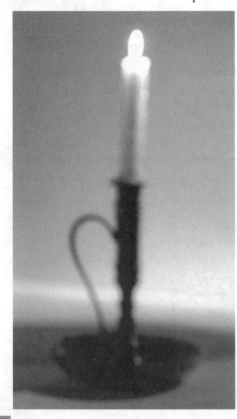

the land of milk and honey. But, the people made an image to characterize the nearness that God had already demonstrated. God promised to be their God—a personal God who would lead them and provide for them. But, the people made an idol of impersonal gold to go before them. God promised to be their God, freed them from Pharaoh to serve God. But, the people made a god and risked becoming slaves to yet another ruler, and a false one at that.

Israel substituted something other than God for God. The result was the exact opposite of what they desired. As they flexed their own muscles, they discovered that they had arrived at the wrong destination. Ironically, however, the golden image illuminated the way to faithfulness and dependence on God.

Look Closer
Read the rest of Exodus 32 to see what happened as a consequence.
Aaron seems to have escaped punishment, but the cost of this sin was
very high. When has some mistake cost you dearly? If you were following a trusted leader and still ran afoul, how did you process that situation? Was there
any added cost?

ARE WE SUBSTITUTING?

Darnell: What's wrong with a visible reminder of God? Does that mean that the cross I wear around my neck is an idol, too?

Daniel: Christians use signs and symbols in worship all the time. Maybe the golden calf was an image used in worship by whoever lived wherever the Israelites were at that moment. Is that any different than me being a Christian and still claiming our reverent use of fire, cedar, and eagle feathers in traditional Native American worship of God? What about our tribal rituals, prayer circles, and cedar ceremonies?

Sanya: My family and I were part of a major midwestern Laotian resettlement program in the late 1970's. My mother died about a year ago. We were the first of the resettled clan to experience death in the United States. We celebrated a Christian

Are We Substituting?
What do you think?
Answer the questions
posed by Darnell,
Daniel, Sanya, and Julie. Are they
substituting something other than
God for God? What are they saying about places, things, voices, or
forces that might delay an exodus
arrival or lead to the wrong destination?

Do you have your own story to
add? What happened and what
did you do? Where was God in
the midst of that event?

service of death and resurrection, but kept all our homeland beliefs and ritual traditions, too. Were we unfaithful?

Julie: We celebrated a reaffirmation of faith for somebody in our church who really turned her life around. Could the melting of the Egyptian gold have just been part of a "homemade" ritual? Maybe they had decided that they would quit complaining and really act like God's chosen ones.

SIT WITH THE WORD

Sit With the Word
Look at these texts from an ironic perspective. Use the "Looking for Irony?" questions on page 63 to study the Scripture narrative. You may choose to spend time with the Scripture individually, in pairs, or in "Break-Out" groups. Limit the focus to just one of the texts.

Read one of the following:
- Matthew 12:1-8
- John 4:5-30, 39-42
- Luke 16:1-9
- Acts 9:1-22

The irony experienced by the Israelites is a great example of God's reality. Irony assumes that reality may actually differ from what appears to be true. Irony makes room for God to be God.

In each of the following narratives, something has been substituted for God; and the human players have either experienced a delay in their exodus arrival or found themselves at the wrong end-point. Engage the Scripture text from an ironic perspective.

The Pharisees

The Pharisees were known as keepers of the Torah Law and Temple requirements. They met Jesus and challenged his interpretation of God's will (Matthew 12:1-8). The Gospels have numerous instances of Jesus' confrontations with the Pharisees, whose office was an honorable one (like seminary professors, for example). But they suffered on occasion from an over-attention to the letter of the Law to the detriment of the spirit of the Law. What might be greater than the Law? Mercy, in the face of human need. The *force* of the Pharisees' faithful zeal led them right out of faith.

A Samaritan Woman

This is the story of a Samaritan woman and Jesus at Jacob's well (John 4:5-30, 39-42). From a Jewish perspective, this well was located in a sort of "enemy territory" among a people who were generally despised by the Jews. Religious tension was compounded by cultural traditions that intimated who could speak to whom, and men usually did not engage unknown women in conversation.

Jesus asked the woman for a drink from the well. The well was a place to satisfy physical thirst. Later, this literal and physical *place* would delay the woman's understanding of Jesus' gift of living water and her call to faithfulness. When she realized that Jesus spoke of spiritual things, she eagerly received his message and spread the word.

SMALL GROUP

Looking for Irony?
- What outcome is desired by the characters involved?
- What contradictions are built-in to this destination?
- What if the opposite of any of the literal facts were really true?
- What part of the narrative appears contrary to what would be reasonable to expect?
- As a distant observer, what do you know that the characters don't?

Discuss the responses together. Where is the irony in each of these narratives? What does the irony tell you about the difference between being religious and being faithful?

The Dishonest Manager

Justice issues related to the possession and accumulation of *things* are complex and cause anxiety for both the "haves" and the "have nots." This parable of the dishonest manager is so honest, when it comes to things, that we simply do not live up to what Jesus asks of his followers (Luke 16:1-9).

The reality is that things cast a shadow on the faithful. Things clearly led the manager to the wrong destination. How is it that he can be both a follower and disobedient at the same time?

Enemy #1

Meet Saul, persecutor and arch-enemy #1 of the church. What happens to enemies of the church? They hear a voice and call that voice *Lord*, right? It is ironic, isn't it? The voice moves from accusation to vocation.

Saul (later Paul) had, in his religious fervor, started out toward Damascus to persecute the Christians. He may have been headed to a right place, but for a wrong reason. For Saul, a *voice* called *Lord* delayed his arrival and terminated his original plans (Acts 9:1-22).

FUSING THE WORD AND MY WORLD

James

You work with James at a graphics design firm. He is very talented and possesses both the charisma and the skill to get the promotions he wants. Your immediate superiors reward him for being out there on the cutting-edge. They say he's confident, dynamic, energetic, spontaneous, and decisive. But, you really dislike working with him. He has no sense of limits or boundaries. Anything goes at whatever cost, and he has to have it all.

Lately you have been watching James pursue Rachelle, the newest employee in your department. You watch as she is showered with his affection and extravagant gifts. You wonder why everybody in the office pays so much attention to her whenever she is on his arm. James seems to be putting all the pieces of the good life together: He has the promotion, the bucks, a girl, a new place. He's got it all!

Yesterday morning you overheard a phone conversation. James was quite agitated. You took two phone messages for James yesterday afternoon—male voice, no name; just a phone number. The same number showed on the answering machine

Fusing the Word and My World

James
What places, things, voices, or forces may be operating in James's life? It doesn't appear that anything slows down James. So if the good life is the right destination, then James has arrived. If it's the wrong destination, how can he get out? How would you define "good life"? Is it a worthy goal to seek? Explain.

Even if a journey is our own, it can have an impact on others. What are some of the possible places, things, or persons who might be influenced by James's decisions and attitudes? What influence does (or can) God have on these places, things, or persons?

after-hours last evening and twice more this morning.

What's going on?

A SECOND CHANCE

After all this desert time of fault-finding, threats, and bargaining by the Israelites, God brings a new force to bear (Exodus 34:1-10). A way out of the wilderness comes as a promise—a forgiving and ever-present God. This is not just a reluctant renewal of what once was, but a new act of God! God made the promise to be a personal, just, merciful, and joy-filled God.

God's promise is not just for the Israelites. The promise is not stuck in time with Abraham and Sarah, Moses and Miriam, Aaron and Joshua. To be ever-present, loving, and forgiving is the way that God is with us in our world.

When have you had a second chance? Your experience may include times when you have been seen some *place* where you never wanted to be caught dead or fell in over your head in a situation due to the *things* in your life. You may have been led by a *voice* that did not care about what happens to you or been torn between the *forces* trying to stake a claim in your life. In times like these, you need to trust God's promise. God shows us a way out and promises another chance.

God makes this promise to us *because* of all the *places*, *things*, *voices*, and *forces* that delay us or lead us away from God. God makes this promise to undergird us, so that we can be faithful and become God's chosen and beloved.

Sound too good to be true? Look for reasons to believe as you tell "second chance" stories to one another. Affirm any experi-

A Second Chance
Read Exodus 34:1-10.
Which of the attributes of God listed in Exodus 34:6-7 can you claim to be true? What would the action of this God mean for you and your situation? What do you still need so that you can believe? What do you still need so that you can live as God's chosen and beloved?

ence of human love or forgiveness as a peek at the awesome love of God. Honestly acknowledge both belief and doubt. If you have been snared by one of those *places*, *things*, *voices*, or *forces*, you might set the scene and trust the group to offer a way to a second chance.

Closer Look: A MAD Group

A small group that focuses on living as God's chosen and beloved could be helpful to you. As Christians, living as God's beloved is discipleship.

Mutual Accountability Discipleship (MAD) groups meet solely for the purpose of nurturing and becoming disciples. MAD groups share respect and power with one another around the table. They are accountable to a common covenant that involves spiritual disciplines, worship, and acts of compassion and justice. MAD group members walk together as God's beloved, as followers of Jesus the Christ.

Once the clauses of the covenant have been identified, MAD groups meet regularly (weekly) for members to give an account of their discipleship. This reporting is done in a nurturing environment that forbids scolding, put-downs, or critical judgment. MAD group members are trustworthy, supportive, and watch over one another in love.

Contact: Bill Crenshaw; 1-877-899-2780 (toll free)
<bcrenshaw@gbod.org>

Resources: By David L. Watson
- *Covenant Discipleship*
- *Forming Christian Disciples*
- *CD Journal: A Guide for Covenant Discipleship Groups on Campus*
  (umsm@gbhem.org)

Going Forth
Use one or more of the following elements for your ritual:
- Scripture: Deuteronomy 30:15-20 (Choosing life as God's faithful)

- Prayer: Prayers of thanksgiving for that which can be believed; or of petition for that which is still needed

- Blessing: Psalm 103:20-22

GOING FORTH

Make use of the leave-taking ritual developed with your group at the end of Session 2.

ARE WE THERE YET?

> This session is designed to affirm and celerate arrival at the end of an exodus trek.

GETTING STARTED

Exodus is a way out. It is a decisive act that leaves behind and moves on. In between a departure and an arrival is a journey that can significantly define the identity and existence of an individual, household, community, or nation.

During the first session, a two-column "Departure/Arrival" chart was made and used to record a list of exodus departure times. Consider each of those departures, and describe possible exodus destinations or arrivals. Record the arrivals in the "Arrivals" column of the chart.

Getting Started
Greet one another. Welcome and identify any newcomers. Invite one another to offer a brief, "life since we last met" update.

WHICH WAY DO WE GO?

After all the years of wandering, the Israelites were on the doorstep of the land of promise! For Israel, this is an arrival. Moses deployed twelve scouts to see for themselves, to spy on the land and people of Canaan (Numbers 13:1-3, 17-33).

Which Way Do We Go?
Read Numbers 13:1-3, 17-33 and Numbers 14. Specifically, what do the Israelites expect from the Promised Land? How will they know that they have arrived?

BIBLE

How do you account for the disparity between what is anticipated by the Israelites and the apparent reality upon arrival at the border of the Promised Land? What happens to those who want to turn back, even now, and to those who are willing to forge ahead?

It is as if a line were drawn in the sand between wilderness and promise. Other lines—lines between old and new, leaders and followers, self and others, and even life and death—are also drawn along the way. When have you experienced this kind of thin-line demarcation between you and your "promised land"?

CASE STUDY

Remember Theresa? How did Theresa get to this threshold of new life? How might she have overcome the negative forces that threatened to pull her back at the very moment she had decided to move on and realize her own promised land?

The reconnaissance report began with fruits from the good, broad land, "flowing with milk and honey." Then, the spies told about the giants that occupied the land in their large and fortified towns. Caleb urged Moses to proceed forward and take the land. The majority refused to press on. Alarmed, the people clamored and complained and called for the selection of a new leader who would lead them back to Egypt (Numbers 14:1-5).

Are we there yet? Israel faced a fork in the road—turn right in trust or turn left in fear. Their majority fear fueled doubt and forced a faint-hearted left to a dead end (Numbers 14). The courageous and faithful few (and the youngest) walked right and would realize God's promises. God's way with God's people would take only forty more years!

Remember Theresa?

Theresa walked out on her partner's regular battering and verbal abuse (see Chapter 1). She had been less than willing to leave, and her reluctance had made her exodus a long time coming. After nearly a year of crying in regret, hiding in fear, and living on the run, Theresa is at the airport waiting to fly to a new job in a new city halfway across the country.

SIT WITH THE WORD

Michelle was chosen to play ball for a university two thousand miles from home. Stefan was caught hiding behind a claim of wealth, a lavish lifestyle, and a pile of credit cards. Brian and his family were forced to leave their home when an explosion and fire ravaged his neighborhood. Kole was accused of sexually abusing a young woman.

Michelle was called out. Stefan was found out. Brian was forced out. Kole was led out. Each left and journeyed from where he or she was to a new reality by way of a wilderness. Now, on the other side of wilderness, their identity and very existence are defined by the consequences of leaving behind, the results of moving on, and the experience of arrival.

Use these "Are We There Yet?" questions throughout the text to study the Scripture narrative. Then, take some time to develop the corresponding scenario.

Are We There Yet?
■ What is the expectation, anticipation, or hope for the end of this exodus trek?
■ How would you use the language of God's salvation—saved, blessed, pardoned, redeemed, delivered, liberated, forgiven, or loved—to describe this arrival experience?
■ How has the identity of the character been defined by the consequences of leaving behind, the results of moving on, and the experience of arrival at the end of this journey?

Sit With the Word
Look at the texts throughout the session and see how each character experiences his or her "promised land" arrival. You may choose to spend time with the Scripture individually, in pairs, or in small groups. You may decide to explore all the texts, choose the one that connects most closely with your own experience, put yourself in God's Promised Land, or divide the texts among "Break-Out" groups.

STILL IN TRANSIT

The Israelites had set up housekeeping in the wilderness of Sinai. Settling down and setting up camp meant preparing a place for the Tabernacle and observing sabbath law. With God who dwelt in their midst, they journeyed on in stages by the command of God to camp or to go on (Numbers 9:15-23). Eventually, after wandering and complaining and dying in the desert, the second generation of the released slaves found their way, with plenty of God's guidance and patience, to the Promised Land.

Still in Transit
Read Numbers 9:15-23, and answer the "Are We There Yet?" questions.

Has some transition or life journey seemed as if it would have no end or resolution? What did that waiting time feel like? What did you do? When an end finally came, how did you experience that? Where did you see God in this time?

For Israel, this is an arrival. This complete dependence on God signals a major transition in the life of this nation. The God who delivered the Israelites from slavery in Egypt is the same God who, with cloud by day and fire by night, will keep the covenant and guide the chosen ones.

Are we there yet? God's covenant with Israel finds them still on the way to the Promised Land, sometimes on pause, other times on fast forward (Deuteronomy 29:10–30:20). Their experiences and hardships helped to insure a clearer vision of how they will continue to make their way.

Look Closer

Look more closely at Deuteronomy 29:10–30:20 for part of a lengthy summary of the Israelites' entry into Canaan. Moses doesn't pull any punches; the people are on the brink of this new and prosperous land completely by the grace of God. At the same time, they live in a covenant not shared by those who worship other gods. What are the benefits and costs of this gift?

CASE STUDY

Remember Michelle?
How did Michelle arrive at this "settling" place? What does it look like? How is it recognized? Whom does she trust to provide her with a guiding system? How will she decide where and when to move on again?

Have you ever taken on a challenge at the urging of someone who had more confidence in you than you did? What was that experience like? What were the consequences? What did you learn? Where did you see God in this time?

Remember Michelle?

Michelle was chosen to play ball for a university two thousand miles from home. Now, five semesters toward her bachelor's degree, she's in her third season with the team, taking major classes, and considering internships.

SET FREE

Hear the outpouring of a heart broken, the lament of one in absolute despair. The psalmist is up to his neck and in the grip of something powerful—his very life is threatened by some impending disaster. Although this one cannot see beyond his own adversity and distress, he keeps praying, believing that God hears, and waiting on God's help (Psalm 69:1-18).

The trouble doesn't end there! The psalmist, while admitting he has done wrong, is apparently the subject of persecution and ridicule for being an enthusiastic supporter of the Temple and service within it (69:9). But if their taunts are believed, the dishonor threatens both the households of faith and of family. He brings humiliation and shame to the people of God and suffers the estrangement of his own kin (69:6-8). The psalmist is a contrite sinner—neither his transgressions nor his regret are hidden. His demonstrative and repentant actions are almost too much. All his enthusiastic and determined efforts to make and keep a right relationship with God just seem to fuel the insults (69:10-12).

Are we there yet? The psalmist prays with confidence and trust in God's grace. Humbled by the hardship he has known, he waits for God's great, faithful love and help—for that abundant mercy that he believes can and will come at any moment (69:13-14).

Remember Stefan?

Stefan is caught hiding behind a claim of wealth, a lavish lifestyle, and a pile of credit cards. No longer able to face the accumulated debt-load, he sees a lawyer and files for bankruptcy. Though the thousands

Set Free
Read Psalm 69:1-18, and answer the "Are We There Yet?" questions on page 69.

Have you ever been judged too harshly or wrongly? Suffered for what you believed and lived out (whether right or wrong)? What was that experience like? What did it teach you? Where did you see God at work in this time?

Remember Stefan?
What happens to the stuff—the cars, the house, and the "finer things in life" when Stefan realizes they possess him rather than the other way around? What happens to the relationships with friends, enemies, employers, credit counsel, and Alise? Bankruptcy marks a definite end, but how is it an arrival for Stefan? How might the humbling task of rebuilding trust on the other side of a personal crash make a way where only formidable obstacles once stood?

Have you ever been buried under the crash of a personal "house of cards"? What happened? What did you learn? Where did you see God at work in that situation?

owed on credit cards are forgiven, Stefan still faces secured student and car loans, a new mortgage, the stigma of bankruptcy, and Alise.

PUT ON THE NEW

Put on the New
Read Ephesians 4:17-32, and answer the "Are We There Yet?" questions on page 69.

Have you ever had to do a dramatic turnaround in your own life? What prompted it? What source of strength did you tap to meet the challenge? Where was God at this time?

Paul appealed to Christians, in the name and authority of Jesus the Christ, to embrace a new reality and live a new life. He contrasted the patterns of old and new to signal the need for a decisive change (Ephesians 4:17-32).

Ephesians 4:22-24 acts as a sort of hinge between what is to be put away and what is to be put on. The dramatic turn is an arrival—a change of heart and mind—rebirth, transformation, conversion.

Are we there yet? For the church at Ephesus (and other churches in Asia Minor), the change of heart and mind is a marker along the way. Becoming the beloved in reality, and actually living out what is put on in Christ, is God's way with God's people.

Remember Brian?
If ignorance is a sign of the old reality, how has the knowledge of methamphetamine informed Brian's new reality? If meth means darkness and death, what does light and life look like? If meth represents bondage, where is the freedom at the end of his temporary exodus?

Have you ever been caught off guard by a serious problem on or near "your turf" that endangered you or your loved ones? What happened? What did you do? What did you learn? Where was God in the midst of this problem?

Remember Brian?

Brian and his family were forced to leave their home when an explosion and fire ravaged his neighborhood. Cleanup is over and rebuilding has commenced, but the old sense of neighborhood is gone. The source of the explosion was a methamphetamine lab. Just knowing that there is meth in the neighborhood has shattered the naiveté that had once been.

DEAD ON ARRIVAL?

The relationship between Moses and the people of Israel culminated at the border between the wilderness and the Promised Land. There was nothing left for Moses to do except actually lead the people into the Promised Land. After guiding, instructing, and interceding for the chosen ones, Moses ended up surveying the land of milk and honey from the mountaintop. That was as close as he got; he was not permitted to enter because of his own sin (see Numbers 20:9-13). Moses' death signaled the end of one era and pointed to the start of the next.

Did Moses fall short of the goal? Was God's promise to Moses left unfulfilled? While Moses' death may be tragic, it was God's way and a turning point—an arrival. The past is decisively over. Moses' death marks the beginning of new leadership through Joshua in a new land of promise (Deuteronomy 34).

Are we there yet? The Book of Deuteronomy ends without the land, but leaves the people poised to realize God's promise. Moses has paved the way to (and beyond!) life in the Promised Land—a way led by God's presence and word in the hearts of the people.

Remember Kole?

Kole was accused of sexually abusing a young woman. Friends and family finally rallied to help him post bond. Kole is living with his family and the binding conditions of his release while he awaits trial. Court documents recording dates, places, and times of alleged contact present some reasonable doubt. But Kole's past is decisively over—regardless of the verdict.

Dead on Arrival? Read Deuteronomy 34, and answer the "Are We There Yet?" questions on page 69.

Have you ever been in a situation like Moses'—so near and yet so far; just on the brink, but not able to cross to the other side of some prized goal? Was it a "failure" or God's way of asking for your trust and patience? How do you know?

Remember Kole? How has Kole been deprived by this accusation? How might either incarceration, probation, or acquittal signal an arrival? How might the verdict initiate a new exodus journey?

Has some problem or tragedy irrevocably changed your life, for better or for worse? What was that like? Where did you see God in the midst of that significant time?

Fusing the Word and My World

Fusing the Word and My World

Summarize by describing and affirming each arrival. Start with the biblical characters. Then, speak specifically about Michelle, Stefan, Brian, or Kole. Compare the different arrival experiences.

Think about your own arrivals and the circumstances in which you arrived. What did you expect from your arrival? How did it compare with the reality of the journey's end?

Reread Ephesians 4:22-24. What do you need to put away in order to move from being to becoming beloved? What do you need to put on to actively live out your belovedness in everything you think, say, and do? How have the consequences of leaving behind, the results of moving on, and your experience of "promised land" arrival influenced your own identity?

Going Forth
Read Deuteronomy 26:1-11. Plan together for your own celebration of first fruits. Design a party that marks just how far you (as a group and personally) have come with God. Set a time and place for food, fellowship, storytelling, and worship. Plan to recall your group's story and claim the specific wealth of God's goodness. Include time to share personal testimonies that witness to the power and blessing of exodus experiences. Celebrate God's way with God's people!

FUSING THE WORD AND MY WORLD

Think about your own exodus story. Compare your "promised land" hopes with that of the biblical characters.

When have you realized that the past was over and done? Focus on your own "hinge" stories.

Think about how your own exodus experiences have shaped you.

GOING FORTH

Just as the festivals of Passover and Unleavened Bread commemorate the deliverance of the Israelites from Pharaoh (Exodus 12:1-28), there is liturgy to celebrate their arrival and the beginning of new life in the land of promise.

The ritual of offering first fruits is a symbolic action of worship, gratitude, and joy. Packed into the celebration is the story of God's promises fulfilled—the land, provisions, and identity that freed the people to serve God and to know abundant life. The liturgical credo moves from the story of God's redemptive and gracious ways with a whole nation to express God's way with each particular one of God's people (Deuteronomy 26:1-11).

Find yourself in this great celebration of salvation. Add yourself to this witness of God's action. Use the language of God's salvation to describe your own "promised land" arrival to other group members. Take your place in this timeless story!

CASE STUDIES

Use any of these cases in place of or in addition to the cases in the sessions as a means of stimulating discussion.

Elan

To be driven off the land, to wander, to move on again and again—that's part of being Cherokee. But now it's personal for Elan. Elan knows his people's ways, but doesn't know who he is. Elan respects other people and their ways, but is afraid of "selling out" to the dominant culture.

Elan sees the poverty, alcohol abuse, and young fatherhood of his brothers; but it is so hard to leave home. Elan knows about the value of a good education, but he really ought to find work that pays.

Elan is caught between going away so that he can "amount to something" and claiming the land and home that belong to him. (Consider this case during Sessions 1 and 7, using the first four questions for Session 1.)

- What are the consequences of leaving behind for Elan? The results of moving on?

- What will it take for exodus to become a viable possibility for Elan?

- What are the connections between faithful living, leaving behind, and moving on? Does Elan go or say no?

- How can Elan discern God's will in his decision?

- Assume that Elan moved on and went away so that he could "amount to something." Where did he go? What did he do? Where did he encounter God?

- What was the expectation, anticipation, or hope for the end of his exodus trek?

- How might Elan have overcome the negative forces that threatened to pull him back?

- How has Elan's identity been defined by the consequences of leaving behind, the results of moving on, and the experience of arrival at the end of his journey?

Kelby

For Kelby, farming is a sustainable, multigenerational family business. Suburban expansion is threatening to convert his tillable farmland to land zoned for commercial use and housing subdivisions. Realtors and developers are offering to resettle Kelby, but they are not paying fair market value for the land. Job Service and other worker employment and training agencies are making promises, but the lifestyle and work is not comparable to life and work on the farm. Kelby begins a hunger strike. (Consider this case with Session 2.)

■ Introduce Kelby's story of displacement to the experience of Lot. How are the circumstances similar? different?

■ The consequences of leaving behind are eliciting a "No go!" from Kelby. When is "No!" a faithful response?

■ We always have choices, even if they all seem unsuitable. How do you sort out when to make the best of a bad situation or to continue the fight? How do you determine when enough is enough? How do you determine what choice God wants for you?

Angel and Carmen (Through Their Translator)

Twelve of us crossed the Mexican border, drove day and night, counting on a promise made by some factory owner in the Midwest. We heard that he had work and some sort of "arrangement" with immigration officials. We're clean—no drugs or anything like that—but, no papers either, and not much English. We showed up and the guy gave us papers. The names and pictures are not ours.

Now what? We could keep working here and risk a hasty deportation. We could stay on at the factory, work on all the legal stuff, and really gamble with deportation. We could move on to a larger metropolitan area where there is extended family and get "lost" awhile. We could go back and try to come into the U.S. legally. The endless possibilities all seem to lead smack into a dead end. (Consider this case with Sessions 3 and 4. The first set of questions is for Session 3.)

■ What are the characteristics of Angel and Carmen's wilderness?

■ What do Angel and Carmen need from an oasis? What would a "miracle of the wilderness" look like to them?

■ Where is their God-given life?

■ How are Angel and Carmen responding to this wilderness trouble?

■ Play out this scenario using patience, trust, and faith—even to the point of personal risk. What happens? Describe the quality of their wilderness waiting in terms of this patience, trust, and faith.

■ As you played this out, who are Angel and Carmen because of this wilderness experience?

Jay-Ann

Jay-Ann says she's just part of the neighborhood. Growing up, she had it better than some, worse than most; was in trouble more than some, less than most; was slower than some, smarter than most; dreamed dreams bigger than some, smaller than most. Just a typical product of the neighborhood and nothing special.

She says lightning struck one day. She got a call that changed her life. She had been working at the corner convenience store that hot Saturday night last summer when a fight started. She had really kept her cool around a bunch of hot-heads. Now some cop was on the phone offering Jay-Ann both training and a real job.

She knew the school police officer and a couple of others on the neighborhood beat. They stopped in the store for coffee almost every day. They talked, and Jay-Ann decided to accept the offer. Jay-Ann had to agree to stay in school, keep her grades up, stay out of trouble, live in the neighborhood, and start to work in the precinct around the corner. In return, Jay-Ann was guaranteed academy training, a job as a police officer, and a chance to make a difference in her neighborhood. (Consider this case with Session 5.)

■ Jay-Ann was chosen! How was the choice made?

■ What were the expectations of the one making the choice?

■ How was Jay-Ann's value or worth influenced by being chosen?

■ What is the cost of being chosen? Could she be "unchosen"? Could she be "unchosen" by God?

Lien

The exodus story of my folks coming to America is not my story! I've heard it a hundred times, but it's not mine! All they've done since they've been here is work so that I could make it here. They worked to show their commitment to our family. They worked so I'd have money for school. Education would bring honor to the family, they said. It would make me a better and more productive member of the family. They worked so that I could contribute to the greater good in this new land.

For years I have heard about who we are. For years we have fought about keeping the language and traditions of home. Whose home? Their home or mine? Make up my mind! They would push and push so that I could make it here and then stand between me and the door.

I thought I'd made a clean break when my neighborhood friends and I went away to college. We had made it—we became totally immersed in the American culture and figured we would never look back. But now, it's all in my face again. My husband and I are going to have a baby, our parents' first grandchild. (Consider this case with Session 6.)

- What places, things, voices, or forces may be operating in Lien's life?

- What outcome does Lien desire?

- What contradictions are built-in to this destination?

- If being totally immersed in the American culture is the right destination, Lien has made it. If it's the wrong destination, how can she "reroute her trip"?

- How can she tell where God wants her to go?

SERVICE LEARNING OPTIONS

New faces, names, and circumstances continue to add to the chronicle of the Exodus story. Consider these service options to help enhance your understanding of exodus.

IDEA #1: Advocate for Immigrants and Refugees

• Sponsor a forum to focus on issues related to immigrants in your area. Invite state and national legislators to discuss systemic economic and social bills and laws that may prevent or discourage large influxes of refugees, migrants, and asylum seekers. See Amnesty International's Web site *www.amnesty.org*

• Become knowledgeable of Immigration and Naturalization Service (INS) work laws. Defend migrants' rights to due process, fair wages, and a safe working environment. Listen to assess their practical needs and respond accordingly. Learn who hires seasonal migrant workers. Initiate a relationship with a migrant family.

• Establish and maintain a "Refugee Welcome Center" that includes a thrift store, food bank, or sanctuary space to care for basic needs. Pool volunteer professionals and translators to provide legal aid, medical care, English-as-a-Second-Language classes, and job training/placement. Organize care (preschool, after-school program, day camp, Vacation Bible School) for the children of immigrant or refugee families.

IDEA #2: Work to Prevent Domestic Abuse

• Compile a library of print and video resources on domestic violence, child abuse, and sexual abuse. Host and recruit leadership for a Sunday morning victim protection series. The series could include an educational component (abuse prevention, detection, and intervention) and a community assessment module (prevention and response resources).

• Arrange meeting space and trained leadership to facilitate peer support groups for battered spouses, adults sexually abused as children, and/or rape victims. Furnish items to a room at a domestic violence center. Offer to connect with the women and children who occupy that room. Listen to the stories that tell of leaving behind, moving on, and hope for new life.